Fondues

Jean Paré

www.companyscoming.com
visit our ↖ website

Front Cover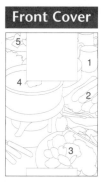

1. Raspberry Punch, page 149
2. Herbed Fondue Bread Sticks, page 87
3. (Vegetable dippers)
4. Chili Con Queso Fondue, page 75
5. (Chip dippers)

Props Courtesy Of:
Stokes
Winners Stores

Back Cover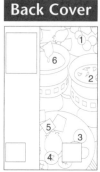

1. (Fruit dippers)
2. Milky Chocolate Fondue, page 98
3. Tiny Ginger Cookies, page 119
4. Peanut Butter Cookies, page 117
5. Crispy Rice Dippers, page 120
6. Cherry Fondue, page 106

Props Courtesy Of:
Stokes
The Bay

Ninth Printing April 2007

Canadian Cataloguing in Publication Data

Paré, Jean
    Fondues : cooking at your table

Includes index.
ISBN 978-1-895455-77-9

    1. Fondue. I. Title. II. Series: Paré, Jean. Original series

TX825.P37 2001   641.8   C2001-901434-1

Published by
Company's Coming Publishing Limited
2311 – 96 Street
Edmonton, Alberta, Canada T6N 1G3
Tel: 780-450-6223   Fax: 780-450-1857
www.companyscoming.com

Company's Coming is a registered trademark owned by Company's Coming Publishing Limited

We acknowledge the financial support of the Government of Canada through the Book Publishing Industry Development Program (BPIDP) for our publishing activities.

Printed in China

Need more recipes?

Six *"sneak preview"* recipes are featured online **with every new book released.**

Visit us at
www.companyscoming.com

Company's Coming Cookbooks

Original Series

- Softcover, 160 pages
- 6" x 9" (15 cm x 23 cm) format
- Lay-flat plastic comb binding
- Full-colour photos
- Nutrition information

Quick & easy recipes! Everyday ingredients!

Lifestyle Series

- Softcover, 160 pages
- 8" x 10" (20 cm x 25 cm) format
- Paperback
- Full-colour photos
- Nutrition information

Most Loved Recipe Collection

- Hardcover, 128 pages
- 8 3/4" x 8 3/4" (22 cm x 22 cm) format
- Durable sewn binding
- Full-colour throughout
- Nutrition information

Special Occasion Series

- Hardcover & softcover
- 8 1/2" x 11" (22 cm x 28 cm) format
- Durable sewn binding
- Full-colour throughout
- Nutrition information

See page 157 for more cookbooks.
For a complete listing, visit
www.companyscoming.com

Table of Contents

The Company's Coming Story . . .   6

Foreword.   7

Fondue Guide   8

Fondue Etiquette And Safety   9

Dipper Selection Guide.   10

Broth Fondues.   11

Oil Fondues.   20

Marinades   46

Dipping Sauces   51

Cheese Fondues   75

Sauce Fondues   94

Dessert Fondues   98

Tabletop Cooking 121

Go-Withs. 141

Measurement Tables 150

Photo Index 151

Tip Index. 152

Recipe Index 153

Mail Order Form 158

What's New! 159

Cookbook Checklist 160

Fondue Guide

Oil Fondues

Marinades

Sauce Fondues

Go-Withs

Tip Index

What's New!

The Company's Coming Story

Jean Paré (pronounced "jeen PAIR-ee") grew up understanding that the combination of family, friends and home cooking is the best recipe for a good life. From her mother, she learned to appreciate good cooking, while her father praised even her earliest attempts in the kitchen. When Jean left home, she took with her a love of cooking, many family recipes and an intriguing desire to read cookbooks as if they were novels!

"never share a recipe you wouldn't use yourself" In 1963, when her four children had all reached school age, Jean volunteered to cater the 50th Anniversary of the Vermilion School of Agriculture, now Lakeland College, in Alberta, Canada. Working out of her home, Jean prepared a dinner for more than 1,000 people, which launched a flourishing catering operation that continued for over 18 years. During that time, she had countless opportunities to test new ideas with immediate feedback—resulting in empty plates and contented customers! Whether preparing cocktail sandwiches for a house party or serving a hot meal for 1,500 people, Jean Paré earned a reputation for good food, courteous service and reasonable prices.

As requests for her recipes mounted, Jean was often asked the question, "Why don't you write a cookbook?" Jean responded by teaming up with her son, Grant Lovig, in the fall of 1980 to form Company's Coming Publishing Limited. The publication of *150 Delicious Squares* on April 14, 1981 marked the debut of what would soon become one of the world's most popular cookbook series.

The company has grown since those early days when Jean worked from a spare bedroom in her home. Today, she continues to write recipes while working closely with the staff of the Recipe Factory, as the Company's Coming test kitchen is affectionately known. There she fills the role of mentor, assisting with the development of recipes people most want to use for everyday cooking and easy entertaining. Every Company's Coming recipe is *kitchen-tested* before it's approved for publication.

Jean's daughter, Gail Lovig, is responsible for marketing and distribution, leading a team that includes sales personnel located in major cities across Canada. In addition, Company's Coming cookbooks are published and distributed under licence in the United States, Australia and other world markets. Bestsellers many times over in English, Company's Coming cookbooks have also been published in French and Spanish.

Familiar and trusted in home kitchens around the world, Company's Coming cookbooks are offered in a variety of formats. Highly regarded as kitchen workbooks, the softcover Original Series, with its lay-flat plastic comb binding, is still a favourite among readers.

Jean Paré's approach to cooking has always called for *quick and easy recipes* using *everyday ingredients*. That view has served her well. The recipient of many awards, including the Queen Elizabeth Golden Jubilee medal, Jean was appointed a Member of the Order of Canada, her country's highest lifetime achievement honour.

Jean continues to gain new supporters by adhering to what she calls The Golden Rule of Cooking: *"Never share a recipe you wouldn't use yourself."* It's an approach that works—millions of times over!

Foreword

Fondues are experiencing a resurgence as people rediscover the simple entertainment of tabletop cooking. Fondue cooking has been around for many years, but guests still feel special when invited over to share in this unique dining experience.

The history of the fondue is not clear, but it would appear that the idea of the communal cooking of meat in one pot probably originated several centuries ago in France and the dunking of stale bread into a mixture of cheese and wine began with the Swiss long ago. Both customs grew out of necessity and poverty. In the 1960s, chocolate fondues were introduced in America. Today, regardless of the type of fondue, it's the social aspect of sitting around the table, sharing from one vessel, which carries this tradition into the twenty-first century.

Fondues includes recipes for oil, broth, cheese, sauce and dessert fondues. Each is distinctive, so you can choose to have a cheese fondue as an appetizer, a broth fondue for your main course and a dessert fondue to end your evening on a sweet note. Or pick one type of fondue as a special highlight for entertaining family or friends. Recipes for other types of tabletop cooking such as the chafing dish, flambé pan and hot stone grill are found in the Tabletop Cooking section.

Fondue cooking means you can spend more time with your guests and less time in the kitchen. Do most of the preparation ahead - cut meats, vegetables and fruit in the morning, make dipping sauces in the afternoon, and set the table with forks, napkins, plates and seasonings before your guests arrive. Then sit back, relax - and join in! With *Fondues* you're ready to let everyone do the cooking!

Each recipe has been analyzed using the most up-to-date version of the Canadian Nutrient File from Health Canada, which is based on the United States Department of Agriculture (USDA) Nutrient Data Base. If more than one ingredient is listed (such as "hard margarine or butter"), or a range is given (1 – 2 tsp., 5 – 10 mL) then the first ingredient or amount is used in the analysis. Where an ingredient reads "sprinkle," "optional," or "for garnish," it is not included as part of the nutrition information. Milk, unless stated otherwise, is 1% and cooking oil, unless stated otherwise, is canola.

Margaret Ng, B.Sc. (Hon), M.A.
Registered Dietitian

Fondue Guide

Using the right equipment is the key to a successful fondue. Below is a brief overview of the different types of fondues and the equipment and tools that work best. Knowing the proper etiquette and safety precautions around the fondue pot also plays a part in everyone enjoying this experience to the fullest. You will also find a chart of suggested dippers, but don't limit yourself to our list. Add your own.

EQUIPMENT

Fondue Pots

The most common types of fondue pots are designed to withstand the high temperatures of hot oil. They are generally made of stainless or porcelainized steel or aluminum and are heated by alcohol fuel or electricity. The top opening is smaller than the base of the pot to ensure that the hot oil will not spatter or splash. They are used for cooking meat, fish and seafood, pastries and battered dippers. These fondue pots can also be used for broth and cheese fondues.

The other types of pots used for cheese fondue are designed to distribute heat evenly at a lower temperature. They are usually made of cast iron or earthenware and heated by liquid or gel fuel. Some cheese fondue pots come with a non-stick coating for easier cleanup.

Small ceramic or earthenware bowls, heated by tea candles to provide very low even heat, are used for sweet sauces such as fruit, caramel and chocolate. The sauce is first made on the stove or in the microwave then transferred to the dessert fondue pot.

The electric fondue pot may lack the romance of a flame, but the adjustable heat source is suitable for all types of sauces, from oil to chocolate.

Fondue Forks

Fondue forks are essential for oil fondues. These long, double-tined metal forks have heat proof handles that are colored in some way so that each person can readily identify which fork is theirs in the pot. Shorter forks are available for cheese and dessert fondues, but regular table forks work well for these too.

Dipping Baskets

Dipping baskets are small wire mesh baskets with long handles. They are only used with oil and broth fondues for scooping out dumplings or small pieces of food that are difficult to retrieve with a fondue fork. A small metal sieve can be used in place of a dipping basket, but for safety reasons it must have a long handle.

Fondue Plates

Individual fondue plates generally have a larger section on which to place the cooked foods and then several smaller sections to hold a variety of dipping sauces. As an alternative, give each guest a regular dinner plate and several small individual ramekins.

Fondue Etiquette And Safety

Fondue is fun, casual and unique. But because there is an open flame, hot oil or other hot liquid, and several people sharing one cooking vessel, there are a number of rules of etiquette and safety that should be followed.

Double Dipping

For hygienic reasons, with all types of fondues but particularly cheese and dessert, we recommend using the fondue fork for dipping only, then using a table fork to pry the morsel onto your own plate for eating. This prevents "double dipping" - dipping, taking a bite and then dipping the same piece of food back into the sauce, or dipping and eating the food item right off the fondue fork then spearing another piece of food and dipping into the sauce.

Location/Setting

You can choose from several possible locations to set up the fondue. Space required depends on the number of people. Generally, you should plan to have one fondue pot for every six people. This is especially important for oil fondues, since the temperature will drop below recommended levels if there is too much food in the pot at one time. Also, too many forks will get tangled and the food can get pulled off when the fork is being removed. In addition, the dipping sauces and go-withs (salads, vegetables and breads) need to be accessible to all or be able to be passed around easily and often. The typical choice for location is the dining room table, especially for a meat or cheese fondue. The coffee table makes a nice setting for a dessert fondue but also works well for a more appetizer-like cheese fondue. But on a warm summer evening, the patio table would be ideal for any of the fondues.

The long history of fondue as a social event has meant the development of certain traditions that you may or may not choose to follow. For example, those who lose their food item or dipper in the fondue pot should be prepared to pay a fine - women traditionally kiss every man at the table while men provide the host with a bottle of wine. If the food is lost a second time, the first person to do so hosts the next fondue party!

Safety

• Read manufacturer's instructions for your fondue set prior to using, especially information on fuel source and cleaning.

• When using an electric fondue, ensure extension cord is taped down to the floor so no one will trip over it.

• When using an oil fondue, keep a fire extinguisher, snuffer lid or box of baking soda handy just in case a flare-up occurs.

• Place fondue pot on a heat proof trivet or small cutting board to protect table surface.

• Control the flame by moving the handle to open or close vents. If all vents are closed, the flame will burn at its lowest.

• Fill burner lamp up to level of wire lattice in a well-ventilated area away from any heat source. Wipe up any spilled fuel. Place lamp on stand and light with match at central opening.

• Extinguish flame by closing vents and putting on snuffer lid. Ensure flame is extinguished before refilling lamp. Lamp should be empty when storing.

• If children participate, an adult should supervise closely to ensure their safety.

• To treat minor burns to fingers from a hot fondue fork, run cold water over burned area, then leave affected area uncovered to quicken healing.

Dipper Selection Guide

Meat	Fish & Seafood	Vegetables
• Beef*	• Clams	• Asparagus
• Deli Meats	• Fish sticks	• Beans
• Ham	• Halibut	• Broccoli
• Lamb*	• Lobster	• Carrots
• Meatballs	• Mussels	• Cauliflower
• Pork*	• Oysters	• Mushrooms
• Sausages	• Scallops	• Parsnips
• Turkey	• Shark	• Pea pods
• Wieners	• Shrimp	• Pearl onions
	• Snapper	• Peppers
* Where possible, choose tender cuts of meat. Freeze for 30 minutes to make cutting easier. Trim fat and gristle. Just prior to cooking, cut meat into bite-size cubes for oil fondues or thin slices for broth fondues. Plan on 4 oz. (113 g) meat per person.	• Squid	• Potato Tots
	• Swordfish	• Potatoes
	• Tuna	• Zucchini

Breads	Cakes & Cookies	Fruit
• Biscuits	• Angel food cake	• Apple
• Bread sticks	• Arrowroot cookies	• Banana
• Corn chips	• Chiffon cake	• Canned mandarin orange segments
• Crackers	• Chocolate cake	
• Cream puffs	• Cream puffs	• Cherries
• Crumpets	• Doughnuts	• Seedless grapes
• Cubed breads such as Black Russian, Brown, French, Italian, Pumpernickel, Rye	• Fig-filled cookies	• Kiwifruit
	• Fruit cake	• Melon
	• Graham wafers	• Orange
• English muffins	• Pound cake	• Pear
• Melba toast	• Shortbread cookies	• Pineapple
• Soda crackers	• Un-iced brownies	• Strawberries
• Spoon-size shredded wheat cereal		
• Toast		
• Tortillas		

Broth Fondues

The Japanese call cooking in a spicy broth "sukiyaki" or "shabu-shabu" while the Chinese call it "ho go" or "huo kuo." Whether you use a plain broth or jazz it up with hot sauce, broth cooking is a low-fat alternative to oil fondues. Depending on the number of people joining in the fondue, and the number of items being cooked, you may need to replenish the broth to keep the level up. All recipes will double and triple easily. In this section we provide a variety of dumplings and other dippers, as well as the usual meat and vegetable accompaniments. At the end of the meal, when all the dippers have flavored the broth, add cooked rice or noodles and serve as a soup. If raw meat was dipped, boil the broth for 5 minutes before adding the rice or noodles.

Beef Hot Pot

An all-in-one fondue complete with suggested dippers and dipping sauces.

Beef tenderloin (or sirloin steak), thinly sliced into strips	1 1/2 lbs.	680 g
SPICY BROTH		
Water	4 cups	1 L
Chicken bouillon powder	2 tsp.	10 mL
Beef bouillon powder	2 tsp.	10 mL
Worcestershire sauce	1 tsp.	5 mL
Ground ginger	1/8 tsp.	0.5 mL
Soy sauce	1 tsp.	5 mL

Roll up each beef strip. Arrange on plate. Cover. Chill.

Spicy Broth: Bring water to a boil in large saucepan. Add remaining 5 ingredients. Stir. Cover. Simmer until ready to fondue. Makes 4 cups (1 L) broth. Carefully pour into fondue pot to no more than 2/3 full. Place over heat high enough to keep broth simmering. Replenish as needed. Spear beef with fondue fork. Cook in broth until desired doneness. Serves 10.

1 serving: 105 Calories; 4.9 g Total Fat; 114 mg Sodium; 14 g Protein; trace Carbohydrate; 0 g Dietary Fiber

Suggested dipping sauces and dippers: Cracked Pepper Sauce, page 51; Kickin' Hot Sauce, page 57; Ginger Sauce, page 69; broccoli florets; cooked baby potatoes; mushrooms.

LAMB HOT POT: Omit beef. Use same amount of very thinly sliced leg of lamb.

Crab Dumplings

Really yummy, with the distinctive flavors of
cream cheese, chili, cayenne and crab.

Finely chopped onion	1/2 cup	125 mL
Cooking oil	1 tsp.	5 mL
Light cream cheese, softened	4 oz.	125 g
Chopped green onion	2 tbsp.	30 mL
Dill weed	1/2 tsp.	2 mL
Lemon juice	1 tsp.	5 mL
Salt	1/4 tsp.	1 mL
Cayenne pepper	1/8 tsp.	0.5 mL
Crabmeat, drained, cartilage removed, flaked (about 1/2 lb., 225 g)	1 2/3 cups	400 mL
Wonton wrappers	77	77
CHICKEN BROTH		
Water	4 cups	1 L
Chicken bouillon powder	4 tsp.	20 mL
Worcestershire sauce	1 tsp.	5 mL

Sauté onion in cooking oil in frying pan until soft. Set aside.

Beat cream cheese in medium bowl until smooth.

Add next 5 ingredients to cream cheese. Mix well.

Add crab and onion to cream cheese mixture. Mix well. Cool.

Cut wonton wrappers into 2 1/2 inch (6.4 cm) circles. Place 1 tsp. (5 mL) crab mixture in center of each circle. Dampen edges with water. Fold over. Pinch edges together to seal. Chill until ready to fondue.

Chicken Broth: Bring water to a boil in large saucepan. Add bouillon powder and Worcestershire sauce. Stir. Cover. Simmer until ready to fondue. Makes 4 cups (1 L) broth. Carefully pour into fondue pot to no more than 2/3 full. Place over heat high enough to keep broth simmering. Replenish as needed. Cook dumplings, a few at a time, in broth for about 2 minutes until dumplings rise to surface. Remove with dipping basket or small metal sieve. Makes 77 dumplings.

(continued on next page)

1 dumpling: 30 Calories; 0.5 g Total Fat; 89 mg Sodium; 1 g Protein; 5 g Carbohydrate; trace Dietary Fiber

Pictured on page 17.

Suggested fondue and dipping sauces: Tartar Sauce, page 66; Spicy Cocktail Sauce, page 67; Sweet And Sour Fondue, page 94.

Shabu-Shabu For Two

SHAH-boo SHAH-boo means "swishing," the sound you hear as the meat is swished through the fondue broth. No need for dipping sauces with this rich broth.

Meat and/or fish, your choice	1/2 lb.	225 g
Vegetables, your choice (see Note)		
RICH CHICKEN BROTH		
Cans of condensed chicken broth	2	2
(10 oz., 284 mL, each)		
Water	1 cup	250 mL

Meats: Choose 3 or more varieties of meat and fish. Cut bite size. Arrange on plate. Cover. Chill until ready to fondue.

Vegetables: Choose as many vegetables as desired. Cut bite size. Arrange on plate. Cover. Chill until ready to fondue.

Rich Chicken Broth: Combine broth and water in large saucepan. Stir. Cover. Simmer until ready to fondue. Makes about 3 cups (750 mL) broth. Carefully pour into electric fondue pot to no more than 2/3 full. Place over heat high enough to keep broth simmering. Replenish as needed.

Spear meat, fish and vegetables with fondue fork. Cook in broth until desired doneness. Serves 2.

1 serving: 563 Calories; 21.9 g Total Fat; 2792 mg Sodium; 35 g Protein; 58 g Carbohydrate; 5 g Dietary Fiber

Note: Vegetables, with the exception of green onions and mushrooms, should be pre-cooked. See Tip, page 21.

 Whatever you cook in a broth will flavor it, leaving you with the base for a very flavorful soup.

Spinach Dumplings

Pretty to look at with a great combination of flavors.
The Vegetable Broth is great to use with Ham Balls, page 19.

Finely chopped onion	1/4 cup	60 mL
Cooking oil	1/2 tsp.	2 mL
Light cream cheese, softened	2 oz.	62 g
Large egg	1	1
Crumbled feta cheese	1/2 cup	125 mL
Low-fat creamed cottage cheese	2 1/2 tbsp.	37 mL
Onion powder	1/8 tsp.	0.5 mL
Dill weed	1/4 tsp.	1 mL
Ground nutmeg	1/16 tsp.	0.5 mL
Salt	1/8 tsp.	0.5 mL
Pepper	1/16 tsp.	0.5 mL
Frozen chopped spinach, thawed and squeezed dry, chopped further	10 oz.	300 g
Wonton wrappers	72	72
VEGETABLE BROTH		
Water	4 cups	1 L
Vegetable bouillon powder	4 tsp.	20 mL

Sauté onion in cooking oil in frying pan until soft. Cool. Set aside.

Beat next 9 ingredients together in medium bowl.

Add spinach and onion. Mix well.

Cut wonton wrappers into 2 1/2 inch (6.4 cm) circles. Place 1 tsp. (5 mL) spinach mixture in center of wrappers. Dampen edges with water. Bring opposite sides together over filling. Pinch edges to seal. Chill until ready to fondue.

Vegetable Broth: Bring water to a boil in large saucepan. Add bouillon powder. Stir. Cover. Simmer until ready to fondue. Makes 4 cups (1 L) broth. Carefully pour into fondue pot to no more than 2/3 full. Place over heat high enough to keep broth simmering. Replenish as needed. Cook dumplings, a few at a time, in broth for about 1 minute until dumplings rise to the surface. Remove with dipping basket or small metal sieve. Makes 72 dumplings.

1 dumpling: 30 Calories; 0.6 g Total Fat; 80 mg Sodium; 1 g Protein; 5 g Carbohydrate; trace Dietary Fiber

Pictured on page 17.

Suggested dipping sauces: Creamy Mint Sauce, page 55; Italian Sauce, page 62; Basil Garlic Mayo, page 64.

Beef Dumplings

Wonderful flavor with a rich blend of spices.
Use the Chicken Broth with Pork Balls, page 16.

Finely chopped onion	1/4 cup	60 mL
Cooking oil	1/2 tsp.	2 mL
Lean ground beef	1/2 lb.	225 g
Egg white (large)	1	1
Chopped chives	1/2 tbsp.	7 mL
Soy sauce	1 tbsp.	15 mL
Sherry (or alcohol-free sherry)	1/2 tbsp.	7 mL
Salt	1/4 tsp.	1 mL
Pepper	1/16 tsp.	0.5 mL
Ground ginger	1/8 tsp.	0.5 mL
Wonton wrappers	64	64
EASY CHICKEN BROTH		
Water	4 cups	1 L
Chicken bouillon powder	4 tsp.	20 mL

Sauté onion in cooking oil in frying pan until soft. Transfer to large bowl.

Add next 8 ingredients. Mix well.

Place 1 tsp. (5 mL) beef mixture in center of each wonton wrapper. Dampen edges with water. Fold over. Pinch edges together to seal. Bring outer 2 corners together at center. Repeat with remaining beef mixture and wonton wrappers. Chill until ready to fondue.

Easy Chicken Broth: Bring water to a boil in large saucepan. Add bouillon powder. Stir. Cover. Simmer until ready to fondue. Makes 4 cups (1 L) broth. Carefully pour into fondue pot to no more than 2/3 full. Place over heat high enough to keep broth simmering. Replenish as needed. Cook dumplings, a few at a time, in broth for about 2 minutes until dumplings rise to the surface. Remove with dipping basket or small metal sieve. Makes 64 dumplings.

1 dumpling: 32 Calories; 0.7 g Total Fat; 85 mg Sodium; 2 g Protein; 5 g Carbohydrate; trace Dietary Fiber

Pictured on page 17.

Suggested dipping sauces: Mustard Sauce, page 64; Cranberry Sauce, page 68; Chutney Curry Sauce, page 70.

Pork Balls

Mildly spicy pork sausage flavor in these golden balls.

Large egg, fork-beaten	1	1
Dry bread crumbs	1/2 cup	125 mL
Garlic powder	1/4 tsp.	1 mL
Onion powder	1/8 tsp.	0.5 mL
Pepper	1/4 tsp.	1 mL
Pork sausage meat	1 lb.	454 g
Chicken Broth, page 12		

Combine first 5 ingredients in medium bowl.

Add sausage meat. Mix well. Shape into 1 inch (2.5 cm) balls. Arrange on plate. Cover. Chill until ready to fondue.

Simmer broth in large saucepan. Carefully pour into fondue pot to no more than 2/3 full. Place over heat high enough to keep broth simmering. Cook pork balls, a few at a time, in broth for about 3 minutes. Remove with dipping basket or small metal sieve. Makes about 62 meatballs.

1 meatball: 15 Calories; 0.5 g Total Fat; 12 mg Sodium; 2 g Protein; 1 g Carbohydrate; trace Dietary Fiber

Pictured on page 54.

Suggested fondue and dipping sauces: Barbecue Sauce, page 52; Rémoulade Sauce, page 59; Mustard Sauce, page 64; Sweet And Sour Fondue, page 94.

1. Snappy Black Bean Sauce, page 60
2. Sesame Sauce, page 69
3. (Vegetable dippers)
4. Crab Dumplings, page 12
5. Beef Dumplings, page 15
6. Spinach Dumplings, page 14

Props Courtesy Of: Le Gnome
Stokes

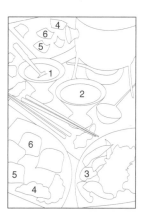

Broth Fondues

Ham Balls

Superb ham flavor with a hint of pickle sweetness.

Large egg	1	1
Dry bread crumbs	3/4 cup	175 mL
Sweet pickle relish	1/4 cup	60 mL
Milk	1/4 cup	60 mL
Ground ham	1 lb.	454 g
Vegetable Broth, page 14		

Combine egg, bread crumbs, relish and milk in medium bowl.

Add ham. Mix well. Shape into 1 inch (2.5 cm) balls. Arrange in single layer on greased baking sheet. Bake in 400°F (205°C) oven for 14 minutes.

Simmer broth in large saucepan. Carefully pour into fondue pot to no more than 2/3 full. Place over heat high enough to keep broth simmering. Warm ham balls, a few at a time, in broth in fondue pot. Makes 72 ham balls.

1 ham ball: 15 Calories; 0.4 g Total Fat; 99 mg Sodium; 2 g Protein; 1 g Carbohydrate; trace Dietary Fiber

Pictured on page 89.

Suggested dipping sauces: Rémoulade Sauce, page 59; Orange Sauce, page 60; Mustard Sauce, page 64; Raisin Honey Sauce, page 73.

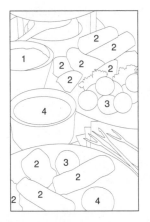

1. Chutney Curry Sauce, page 70
2. Fried Cheese, page 32
3. Reuben Gems, page 22
4. Marmalade Fondue, page 111

Props Courtesy Of: Pfaltzgraff Canada
Stokes

Oil Fondues

Oil fondues cook meat, vegetables and pastries to perfection. In particular, meat done in cooking oil is very flavorful. For a complete meal, serve a meat fondue with several dipping sauces, a salad and bread sticks. As an added attraction, have on hand a batter or coating (pages 38 and 39) for dipping fresh vegetables.

Preheat cooking oil in fondue pot on the stove to 375°F (190°C). We strongly recommend using a candy thermometer to determine the temperature; however, for a quick test, a cube of bread should brown in 40 to 60 seconds. For safety reasons, the fondue pot should be no more than two-thirds full of cooking oil. Place fondue pot on stand over high heat. We tested all our recipes with canola oil, but peanut oil also worked well and has a higher smoke point. If the cooking oil does start to smoke, remove from heat for a few minutes. If the cooking oil cools too much, just return to the stove to heat to the desired temperature.

Basic Oil Fondue

For a simple fondue, mix and match your choice of meat, poultry, fish or seafood for a total of 1 1/2 lbs. (680 g) to serve 6 people. Fill fondue pot to no more than 2/3 full with cooking oil. Heat on stove to 375°F (190°C). Transfer fondue pot to stand over heat high enough to maintain cooking oil at 375°F (190°C).

Pictured on page 71.

Beef

Use: Beef tenderloin, cubed

Cooking time: About 20 seconds for rare; 30 seconds for medium; 40 seconds for well done.

4 oz. (113 g) beef: 296 Calories; 21 g Total Fat; 63 mg Sodium; 24 g Protein; 2 g Carbohydrate; trace Dietary Fiber

Suggested dipping sauces: Cracked Pepper Sauce, page 51; Snappy Black Bean Sauce, page 60.

Chicken

Use: Boneless, skinless chicken breast halves, cubed

Cooking time: About 2 minutes until no longer pink inside.

(continued on next page)

4 oz. (113 g) chicken: 253 Calories; 14.7 g Total Fat; trace Sodium; 26 g Protein; 3 g Carbohydrate; trace Dietary Fiber

Suggested dipping sauces: Basil Garlic Mayo, page 64; Lemon Caper Butter, page 66.

Fish & Seafood

Use: Shrimp, scallops, etc. (or any firm fish), cubed

Cooking time: Most fish and seafood will take 30 seconds.

4 oz. (113 g) shrimp: 115 Calories; 1.8 g Total Fat; 137 mg Sodium; 22 g Protein; 1 g Carbohydrate; 0 g Dietary Fiber

Suggested dipping sauces: Tartar Sauce, page 66; Spicy Cocktail Sauce, page 67.

Pork

Use: Pork tenderloin (or ham), cubed

Cooking time: About 1 minute until no longer pink inside.

4 oz. (113 g) pork tenderloin: 278 Calories; 19.9 g Total Fat; 57 mg Sodium; 23 g Protein; 0 g Carbohydrate; 0 g Dietary Fiber

Suggested dipping sauces: Orange Sauce, page 60; Ginger Sauce, page 69.

Lamb

Use: Leg of lamb, cubed

Cooking time: About 1 minute until no longer pink inside.

4 oz. (113 g) lamb: 145 Calories; 5.1 g Total Fat; 70 mg Sodium; 23 g Protein; 0 g Carbohydrate; 0 g Dietary Fiber

Suggested dipping sauces: Creamy Mint Sauce, page 55; Chutney Curry Sauce, page 70.

Certain vegetables, such as broccoli, carrots and cauliflower, should be cooked until tender-crisp before cooking in broth or oil fondues. Potatoes will cloud a broth fondue if not precooked. Mushrooms, peppers, green onions and zucchini are best cooked from the raw state in a fondue pot.

Reuben Gems

*The unmistakable flavor of sauerkraut
in a creamy base makes this dipper a hit.*

Cream cheese, softened	4 oz.	125 g
Canned corned beef (1/2 of 12 oz., 340 g, can), drained and chopped	6 oz.	170 g
Sweet pickle relish	1 tbsp.	15 mL
Onion powder	1/4 tsp.	1 mL
Can of sauerkraut, drained, chopped and blotted dry	14 oz.	398 mL
MUSTARD COATING		
Prepared mustard	3 tbsp.	50 mL
Water	6 tbsp.	100 mL
Fine dry bread crumbs	2/3 cup	150 mL
Cooking oil, for fondue pot (no more than 2/3 full)		

Mash cream cheese with fork in medium bowl. Add corned beef, relish, onion powder and sauerkraut. Mash together. Shape mixture into 1 inch (2.5 cm) balls.

Mustard Coating: Combine mustard and water in small cup.

Put bread crumbs into small bowl. Dip each ball into mustard mixture. Roll in bread crumbs to coat completely. Chill until firm.

Cook balls, a few at a time, in hot (375°F, 190°C) cooking oil in fondue pot for 1 minute until golden. Remove with dipping basket or small metal sieve. Makes 40 balls.

1 ball: 38 Calories; 2.6 g Total Fat; 121 mg Sodium; 2 g Protein; 2 g Carbohydrate; trace Dietary Fiber

Pictured on page 18.

Suggested fondue and dipping sauces: Orange Sauce, page 60; Mustard Sauce, page 64; Marmalade Fondue, page 111.

Meatballs

Moist and flavorful with a hint of barbecue sauce. Use with oil or broth fondues.

Large egg, fork-beaten	1	1
Beef bouillon powder	1 tsp.	5 mL
Worcestershire sauce	1 tsp.	5 mL
Finely chopped onion	1/3 cup	75 mL
Dry bread crumbs	1/2 cup	125 mL
Water	1/4 cup	60 mL
Barbecue sauce	1 tbsp.	15 mL
Salt	3/4 tsp.	4 mL
Pepper	1/4 tsp.	1 mL
Lean ground beef	1 lb.	454 g

Cooking oil, for fondue pot (no more than 2/3 full)

Combine first 9 ingredients in medium bowl. Stir.

Add ground beef. Mix well. Shape into 3/4 inch (2 cm) balls. Arrange on large plate. Cover. Chill until ready to fondue.

Spear meatballs with fondue fork. Cook meatballs, a few at a time, in hot (375°F, 190°C) cooking oil in fondue pot for about 3 minutes until no pink remains in meatball. Makes about 74 meatballs.

1 meatball: 25 Calories; 1.8 g Total Fat; 46 mg Sodium; 1 g Protein; 1 g Carbohydrate; trace Dietary Fiber

Pictured on page 54.

Suggested fondues and dipping sauces: Barbecue Sauce, page 52; Rémoulade Sauce, page 59; Teriyaki Sauce, page 61; Italian Sauce, page 62; Plum Sauce, page 68; Raisin Honey Sauce, page 73; Sweet And Sour Fondue, page 94; Appetizer Fondue, page 95; Beer Fondue, page 96; Creamy Curry Fondue, page 96.

 Rub herbs into meat at least one hour before cooking. Sprinkling herbs onto meat just before cooking will result in the herbs burning off and not flavoring the meat.

A Snap Fondue

A package of frozen appetizers makes this fondue a snap.
Easy to enlarge by using different varieties.

Package of frozen deep-fried Oriental hors d'oeuvres (or canapés)	10 oz.	285 g

Cooking oil, for fondue pot (no more
than 2/3 full)

Arrange frozen hors d'oeuvers on plates. Cover. Thaw in refrigerator.

Cook hors d'oeuvers, a few at a time, in hot (375°F, 190°C) cooking oil in fondue pot for about 1 minute until golden. Remove with dipping basket or small metal sieve. Makes about 16 appetizers.

*1 appetizer: 73 Calories; 4.6 g Total Fat; 220 mg Sodium; 2 g Protein; 6 g Carbohydrate;
0 g Dietary Fiber*

Suggested dipping sauces: Mustard Sauce, page 64; Tartar Sauce, page 66; Spicy Cocktail Sauce, page 67; Plum Sauce, page 68.

 To avoid contamination on a platter, separate meat, fish and vegetables with fresh herbs or parsley or use individual plates.

Seasoned Calamari

Crispy coating contrasts the tender Calamari.
Can be coated and chilled up to 2 hours ahead of time.

Large egg, fork-beaten	1	1
Lemon juice	1 tsp.	5 mL
Seasoned salt	1/2 tsp.	2 mL
Cayenne pepper	1/2 tsp.	2 mL
Garlic powder	1/4 tsp.	1 mL
Onion powder	1/4 tsp.	1 mL
Cornstarch	2 tbsp.	30 mL
Squid tubes	8 oz.	225 g
Fine dry bread crumbs	1/2 cup	125 mL
Cooking oil, for fondue pot (no more than 2/3 full)		

Combine egg, lemon juice, seasoned salt, cayenne pepper, garlic powder and onion powder in medium bowl. Stir.

Stir in cornstarch until smooth.

Pat squid dry. Cut into 1/4 inch (6 mm) slices. Add to egg mixture. Stir until well coated.

Roll squid in bread crumbs to coat completely. Arrange on plate. Cover. Chill until ready to fondue.

Cook squid, a few at a time, in hot (375°F, 190°C) cooking oil in fondue pot until golden. Remove with dipping basket or small metal sieve. Makes about 40 rings.

1 ring: 36 Calories; 2.6 g Total Fat; 32 mg Sodium; 1 g Protein; 2 g Carbohydrate; trace Dietary Fiber

Variation: Squid tubes can also be cut down one side, opened and cut into diamonds or squares.

Suggested dipping sauces: Aïoli Sauce, page 56; Madeira Butter Sauce, page 65; Lemon Caper Butter, page 66.

Tempura Fondue

A light and crispy batter that allows the flavor of the food to come through.

TEMPURA BATTER

Egg yolk (large)	1	1
Ice water	2 cups	500 mL
All-purpose flour	1 2/3 cups	400 mL
Baking soda	1/8 tsp.	0.5 mL
All-purpose flour	2 tsp.	10 mL
Medium shrimp, peeled and deveined, tail intact	18	18
Thin red snapper (or sole or orange roughy or plaice) fillets, cubed	6	6
Boneless, skinless chicken breast halves (about 1 lb., 454 g), cubed	4	4
Small eggplant, with peel, cut into wedges	1	1
Whole fresh mushrooms, halved	9	9
Medium green or red pepper, cut into 12 chunks	1	1
Daikon radish, thinly sliced	1	1
Sweet potatoes, thinly sliced (see Note)	1/2 lb.	225 g
Potatoes, thinly sliced (see Note)	1/2 lb.	225 g
Cooking oil, for fondue pot (no more than 2/3 full)		

Tempura Batter: Beat egg yolk and ice water together in medium bowl. Add first amount of flour and baking soda. Stir until just moistened. Do not overmix. Batter should have lumps of dry flour.

Use second amount of flour to dust next 9 ingredients. Arrange on plates. Spear individual pieces with fondue fork. Dip into batter to coat completely.

Cook in hot (375°F, 190°C) cooking oil in fondue pot until golden. Serves 6.

1 serving: 671 Calories; 24 g Total Fat; 208 mg Sodium; 58 g Protein; 53 g Carbohydrate; 5 g Dietary Fiber

(continued on next page)

Pictured on page 35.

Suggested dipping sauces: Cream Cheese Sauce, page 40; Bacon Blue Cheese Sauce, page 62; Dilly-Of-A-Dipping Sauce, page 67.

Note: Canned sweet potatoes and potatoes may be used. Or cut the fresh potato into thick slices and partially cook on the stove for about 10 minutes until fork tender.

Potato Skins

A traditional appetizer prepared in a novel way.

Large baking potatoes, baked and cooled	3	3
Seasoned salt, sprinkle		
Cooking oil, for fondue pot (no more than 2/3 full)		

Cut potatoes in half lengthwise. Scoop out potato, leaving shell about 1/4 inch (6 mm) thick. Cut each shell crosswise into 1 inch (2.5 cm) wide strips. Sprinkle with seasoned salt. Arrange on plate. Cover. Chill until ready to fondue.

Cook potato skins, a few at a time, in hot (375°F, 190°C) cooking oil in fondue pot until crisp and golden. Remove with dipping basket or small metal sieve. Makes 30 potato skins.

1 potato skin: 22 Calories; 1.2 g Total Fat; 1 mg Sodium; trace Protein; 3 g Carbohydrate; trace Dietary Fiber

 Always fondue on a level table or other flat surface to avoid spillage. If the fondue pot doesn't come with a heat-resistant trivet, use a hot pad, wooden cutting board or ceramic tile to protect the table surface.

Samosas

Always a delight, these golden triangles originating from India have a slightly spicy flavor.

Small onion, finely chopped	1	1
Cooking oil	1 tsp.	5 mL
Cooked mashed potatoes	1/2 cup	125 mL
Cooked peas	1/4 cup	60 mL
Lemon juice	1/2 tsp.	2 mL
Garlic powder	1/8 tsp.	0.5 mL
Chili powder	1/4 tsp.	1 mL
Ground ginger	1/4 tsp.	1 mL
Ground cumin	1/16 tsp.	0.5 mL
Salt	1/4 tsp.	1 mL
Pepper	1/8 tsp.	0.5 mL
Parsley flakes	1 1/2 tsp.	7 mL
Chopped green onion	1 1/2 tsp.	7 mL

Pastry for 2 crust pie, your own or
 a mix

Cooking oil, for fondue pot (no more
 than 2/3 full)

Sauté onion in first amount of cooking oil in frying pan until soft. Remove from heat.

Add next 11 ingredients. Mix well.

Roll out pastry on lightly floured surface. Cut into 3 inch (7.5 cm) circles. Cut circles in half. Place 1/2 tsp. (2 mL) potato mixture in center of each half. Dampen edges with water. Fold over, matching edges. Press edges together with floured fork or pinch to seal. Arrange on plates. Cover. Chill until ready to fondue.

Cook samosas, a few at a time, in hot (375°F, 190°C) cooking oil in fondue pot for 2 to 2 1/2 minutes, turning to brown both sides. Remove with dipping basket or small metal sieve. Makes about 60 samosas.

1 samosa: 64 Calories; 4.3 g Total Fat; 84 mg Sodium; 1 g Protein; 6 g Carbohydrate; trace Dietary Fiber

Pictured on page 54.

Pups In Blankets

A perfect amount of batter to coat 1 lb. (454 g) wieners in a golden crust. Children will really like these little nuggets. Freeze or chill the leftovers for a snack another day.

Wieners (12 per package size), cut into 6 pieces each	1 lb.	454 g

Basic Batter, page 38

Cooking oil, for fondue pot (no more than 2/3 full)

Spear wiener with fondue fork. Dip into batter to coat completely.

Cook, a few at a time, in hot (375°F, 190°C) cooking oil in fondue pot for about 1 1/2 minutes until puffed and golden. Makes 72 pups in blankets.

1 pup in blanket: 38 Calories; 2.7 g Total Fat; 92 mg Sodium; 1 g Protein; 2 g Carbohydrate; trace Dietary Fiber

Pictured on page 36.

Suggested fondue and dipping sauces: Barbecue Sauce, page 52; Mustard Sauce, page 64; Sweet And Sour Fondue, page 94.

 To prevent food, especially meat, from sticking to the bottom of the fondue pot, move the food periodically during cooking.

Falafels

Feh-LAH-fehls are a specialty from the Middle East with
delicate spicing and a pleasant after-nip.

Can of chick peas (garbanzo beans), drained and liquid reserved	19 oz.	540 mL
Medium onion, coarsely chopped	1	1
Reserved chick pea liquid	2 – 3 tbsp.	30 – 50 mL
Ground cumin	1/2 tsp.	2 mL
Garlic powder	1/2 tsp.	2 mL
Baking soda	1 tsp.	5 mL
Cayenne pepper	1/4 tsp.	1 mL
Salt	1/2 tsp.	2 mL
Pepper	1/8 tsp.	0.5 mL
Parsley flakes	1 tsp.	5 mL
Large egg, fork-beaten	1	1
Fine dry bread crumbs	1 cup	250 mL

Cooking oil, for fondue pot (no more than 2/3 full)

Put chick peas and onion in food processor. Purée, adding enough reserved liquid, until smooth.

Combine next 9 ingredients in medium bowl. Add chick pea mixture. Stir well. Shape into 3/4 inch (2 cm) balls. Arrange on plate. Cover. Chill until ready to fondue.

Cook falafels, a few at a time, in hot (375°F, 190°C) cooking oil in fondue pot until browned. Remove with dipping basket or small metal sieve. Makes about 70 falafels.

1 falafel: 24 Calories; 1 g Total Fat; 74 mg Sodium; 1 g Protein; 3 g Carbohydrate; trace Dietary Fiber

Pictured on page 54.

Suggested dipping sauces: Creamy Mint Sauce, page 55; Yogurt Cuke Sauce, page 58; Creamy Avocado Dip, page 58; Mustard Sauce, page 64.

Variation: Deep-fry falafels ahead of time, in 2 batches. Serve as dippers with dipping sauces.

Mixed Veggies

Beautiful golden morsels with a fabulous fresh vegetable taste.

Mixed peppers (green, red and yellow), cut into squares	3	3
Small whole fresh mushrooms	1 lb.	454 g
Partially cooked cubed potato	1 lb.	454 g

Crumb Coating, page 37 (or Crispy
    Crumb Coating, page 38)
Basic Batter, page 38

Cooking oil, for fondue pot (no more
    than 2/3 full)

Arrange peppers, mushrooms and potato on plates. Spear vegetable with fondue fork.

Roll vegetable in coating, or dip into batter to coat completely.

Cook veggies, in hot (375°F, 190°C) cooking oil in fondue pot until golden. Serves 8.

1 serving: 343 Calories; 16.1 g Total Fat; 895 mg Sodium; 12 g Protein; 39 g Carbohydrate; 4 g Dietary Fiber

Suggested dipping sauces: Cracked Pepper Sauce, page 51; Creamy Avocado Sauce, page 58; Italian Sauce, page 62; Dilly-Of-A-Dipping Sauce, page 67.

Paré Pointer
They thought Joan of Arc was Noah's wife.

Fried Cheese

Certain to become one of your favorite dippers.

Large eggs	3	3
Fine dry bread crumbs	1 cup	250 mL
Salt	1/2 tsp.	2 mL
Pepper	1/8 tsp.	0.5 mL
Paprika	1/4 tsp.	1 mL
Assorted cheese (Cheddar, Gouda, mozzarella), cut into 3/4 inch (2 cm) cubes	1 lb.	454 g
Cooking oil, for fondue pot (no more than 2/3 full)		

Beat eggs well in small bowl.

Combine next 4 ingredients in separate small bowl.

Dip cheese into egg. Roll in crumb mixture to coat. Repeat coatings. Arrange on plate. Cover. Chill until ready to fondue.

Cook cheese cubes, a few at a time, in hot (375°F, 190°C) cooking oil in fondue pot for about 20 seconds until golden. Remove with dipping basket or small metal sieve. Makes about 60 pieces.

1 piece: 45 Calories; 3.3 g Total Fat; 87 mg Sodium; 2 g Protein; 2 g Carbohydrate; trace Dietary Fiber

Pictured on page 18.

Suggested dipping sauces: Kickin' Hot Sauce, page 57; Niçoise Sauce, page 63; Chutney Curry Sauce, page 70.

Paré Pointer

Flattery is wonderful. It's like perfume, to be sniffed but not swallowed.

Garlic Dipping Squares

Crisp and golden on the outside, soft on the inside!

Large eggs	2	2
Hard margarine (or butter), melted	2 tbsp.	30 mL
Water	1 tbsp.	15 mL
Garlic powder	1 tbsp.	15 mL
French bread slices, cut 1 inch (2.5 cm) thick	4	4
Parmesan cheese	1/2 cup	125 mL
Cooking oil, for fondue pot (no more than 2/3 full)		

Beat eggs well in small bowl.

Add margarine, water and garlic powder. Stir.

Cut bread into 1 inch (2.5 cm) cubes. Dip into egg. Roll in cheese to coat completely. Chill for at least 1 hour.

Spear cubes with fondue fork. Cook, a few at a time, in hot (375°F, 190°C) cooking oil in fondue pot until crisp and golden. Makes 36 squares.

1 square: 35 Calories; 2.3 g Total Fat; 62 mg Sodium; 1 g Protein; 2 g Carbohydrate; trace Dietary Fiber

Suggested dipping sauces: Cream Cheese Sauce, page 40; Bacon Blue Cheese Sauce, page 62; Dilly-Of-A-Dipping Sauce, page 67.

For broth fondues, slice meat paper thin against the grain so it cooks quickly. Cubed meat works well for oil fondues since the outer layer sears quickly to keep in all the juices.

Stuffing Coating

A coating that tastes like stuffing.

Large egg	1	1
Water	2 tsp.	10 mL
Fine dry bread crumbs	1 cup	250 mL
Parsley flakes	1/2 tsp.	2 mL
Poultry seasoning	1/2 tsp.	2 mL
Onion powder	1/2 tsp.	2 mL
Salt	1/4 tsp.	1 mL
Pepper	1/8 tsp.	0.5 mL
Paprika	1/4 tsp.	1 mL

Beat egg and water together in small bowl.

Combine remaining 7 ingredients in separate small bowl. Makes about 1 cup (250 mL) coating. Dip food into egg mixture. Roll in crumb mixture to coat completely. Arrange on plate. Cover. Chill until ready to fondue.

1 tbsp. (15 mL) coating plus 1/16 egg and water mixture: 33 Calories; 0.7 g Total Fat; 103 mg Sodium; 1 g Protein; 5 g Carbohydrate; trace Dietary Fiber

Suggested food to coat: Boneless, skinless chicken breast cubes; pork tenderloin cubes.

1. Tempura Fondue, page 26
2. Ginger Sauce, page 69
3. Tartar Sauce, page 66
4. (Vegetable dippers)

Props Courtesy Of: Pfaltzgraff Canada
Stokes

Crumb Coating

A touch of color and flavor from the paprika.

Large eggs	2	2
Water	4 tsp.	20 mL
Fine dry bread crumbs	1 cup	250 mL
Paprika	1 tsp.	5 mL
Seasoned salt	2 tsp.	10 mL
Cajun seasoning	1/2 tsp.	2 mL

Beat eggs and water together in small bowl.

Combine bread crumbs, paprika, seasoned salt and cajun seasoning in separate small bowl. Makes 1 cup (250 mL) coating. Dip food into egg mixture. Roll in crumb mixture to coat completely. Arrange on plate. Cover. Chill until ready to fondue.

1 tbsp. (15 mL) coating plus 1/16 egg and water mixture: 38 Calories; 1.1 g Total Fat; 219 mg Sodium; 2 g Protein; 5 g Carbohydrate; trace Dietary Fiber

Suggested food to coat: Mixed Veggies, page 31; boneless, skinless chicken breast cubes; fish fillets; assorted vegetable chunks.

1. (Chicken with) Ginger Marinade, page 49
2. Black Currant Fondue, page 112
3. Basic Batter, page 38
4. Pups In Blankets, page 29
5. Cracked Pepper Sauce, page 51
6. Barbecue Sauce, page 52
7. (Vegetable dippers)

Props Courtesy Of: Cherison Enterprises Inc.
Stokes

Crispy Crumb Coating

A lightly seasoned coating with a hint of Parmesan cheese.

Large eggs	3	3
Water	3 tbsp.	50 mL
Fine dry bread crumbs	1 cup	250 mL
Grated Parmesan cheese	1/3 cup	75 mL
Parsley flakes	1/2 tsp.	2 mL
Paprika	1/2 tsp.	2 mL
Salt	3/4 tsp.	4 mL
Pepper	1/4 tsp.	1 mL

Beat eggs and water together in small bowl.

Combine bread crumbs, Parmesan cheese, parsley, paprika, salt and pepper in separate small bowl. Makes about 1 1/2 cups (375 mL) coating. Dip food into egg mixture. Roll in crumb mixture to coat completely. Arrange on plate. Cover. Chill until ready to serve.

1 tbsp. (15 mL) coating plus 1/25 egg and water mixture: 34 Calories; 1.3 g Total Fat; 144 mg Sodium; 2 g Protein; 3 g Carbohydrate; trace Dietary Fiber

Suggested food to coat: Mixed Veggies, page 31; boneless, skinless chicken breast cubes; sirloin steak cubes; assorted vegetable and cheese chunks.

Basic Batter

An all-purpose batter that coats almost any food.

Large egg	1	1
Cooking oil	1 1/2 tbsp.	25 mL
Milk	7/8 cup	200 mL
All-purpose flour	1 cup	250 mL
Granulated sugar	1 tsp.	5 mL
Baking powder	2 tsp.	10 mL
Salt	1/2 tsp.	2 mL
Onion powder	1/2 tsp.	2 mL

(continued on next page)

Oil Fondues

Beat egg and cooking oil together in medium bowl. Add milk. Stir.

Add remaining 5 ingredients. Beat until smooth. Add a bit more milk if batter is too stiff or a bit more flour if too thin. Makes 1 2/3 cups (400 mL).

1 tbsp. (15 mL): 32 Calories; 1.2 g Total Fat; 76 mg Sodium; 1 g Protein; 4 g Carbohydrate; trace Dietary Fiber

Pictured on page 36.

Suggested food to coat: Pups In Blankets, page 29; Mixed Veggies, page 31.

Quick Batter

An easy way to get a crunchy coating on just about any food you would want to cook in a fondue pot.

Pancake mix	1 cup	250 mL
Ginger ale (or water)	1 cup	250 mL

Combine pancake mix and ginger ale in medium bowl. Stir until smooth, adding more ginger ale to thin as needed. Batter won't coat well if too stiff. Stir batter for 1 to 2 minutes to remove excess bubbles. Makes 1 1/2 cups (375 mL).

1 tbsp. (15 mL): 24 Calories; 0.3 g Total Fat; 67 mg Sodium; 1 g Protein; 5 g Carbohydrate; trace Dietary Fiber

Pictured on page 53.

QUICK CRUMBED BATTER: Coat food with batter. Roll in fine dry bread crumbs.

 Batter will cling better if the food is dusted with flour first.

Tropical Fondue

Everyone will enjoy this reminder of a vacation in paradise. The Cream Cheese Sauce can also be used with Garlic Dipping Squares, page 33.

CREAM CHEESE SAUCE

Light cream cheese, softened	4 oz.	125 g
Icing (confectioner's) sugar	2 cups	500 mL
Vanilla	1 tsp.	5 mL
Milk	3 tbsp.	50 mL
Graham cracker crumbs (optional)	1 cup	250 mL

FRITTER BATTER

All-purpose flour	1 cup	250 mL
Granulated sugar	2 tbsp.	30 mL
Cornstarch	1 tbsp.	15 mL
Baking powder	1 tsp.	5 mL
Salt	1/2 tsp.	2 mL
Milk	1 cup	250 mL
Can of pineapple chunks, drained, patted dry	14 oz.	398 mL
Medium bananas, sliced 1/2 inch (12 mm) thick	2	2
All-purpose flour, for dusting	1 tbsp.	15 mL
Cooking oil, for fondue pot (no more than 2/3 full)		

Cream Cheese Sauce: Beat cream cheese, gradually adding icing sugar until fully incorporated.

Add vanilla and milk. Beat until smooth. Divide among individual small bowls.

Divide graham crumbs among individual small bowls.

Fritter Batter: Combine first 6 ingredients in medium bowl. Beat until smooth. Place beside fondue pot and plate of fruit.

Dust fruit with flour. Spear with fondue fork. Dip into batter to coat completely. Cook in hot (375°F, 190°C) cooking oil in fondue pot until puffed and golden. Cool slightly. Dip into sauce, then into graham crumbs. Serves 6.

1 serving: 446 Calories; 11.1 g Total Fat; 418 mg Sodium; 6 g Protein; 82 g Carbohydrate; 2 g Dietary Fiber

Fruit Packets

Golden triangle packages bursting with a colorful fruit filling.
Sweet and crunchy in the same bite.

Package of refrigerator crescent-style rolls (8 rolls per tube)	8 1/2 oz.	235 g
Mixed glazed fruit	1/4 cup	60 mL
Chopped dark raisins	2 tbsp.	30 mL
Chopped pecans	2 tbsp.	30 mL
Liquid honey	1 tbsp.	15 mL

Cooking oil, for fondue pot (no more than 2/3 full)

Icing (confectioner's) sugar, for dusting

Separate crescent rolls. Cut each into 2 equal triangles.

Combine mixed fruit, raisins, pecans and honey in small bowl. Place 1 1/2 tsp. (7 mL) fruit mixture in center of each triangle. Fold pastry over fruit to form smaller triangle. Press edges together with floured fork or pinch to seal.

Cook packets, a few at a time, in hot (375°F, 190°C) cooking oil in fondue pot for 2 minutes, turning at halftime to brown other side. Remove with dipping basket or small metal sieve.

Dust with icing sugar. Makes 16 packets.

1 packet: 73 Calories; 4.2 g Total Fat; 143 mg Sodium; 1 g Protein; 8 g Carbohydrate; trace Dietary Fiber

---

Paré Pointer

She got her good looks from her father. He's a plastic surgeon.

Perogy Fruit Pies

Careful of that first bite—it will be very hot.

FRUIT FILLING

Water	1 tsp.	5 mL
Cornstarch	1 tsp.	5 mL
Commercial pie filling (your choice), stir before dividing, chop large pieces	3/4 cup	175 mL

PASTRY

All-purpose flour	1 cup	250 mL
Baking powder	1/4 tsp.	1 mL
Salt	1/4 tsp.	1 mL
Warm water, approximately	6 tbsp.	100 mL

Cooking oil, for fondue pot (no more than 2/3 full)

Icing (confectioner's) sugar, for dusting

Fruit Filling: Stir water into cornstarch in small bowl until smooth. Add pie filling. Stir well.

Pastry: Combine flour, baking powder and salt in medium bowl or food processor. Mix in warm water, 1 tbsp. (15 mL) at a time, until stiff dough forms. Turn out onto lightly floured surface. Knead until smooth. Wrap in plastic wrap. Let rest at room temperature for 15 to 30 minutes until dough is softened. Roll out 1/2 of dough on lightly floured surface to 1/16 inch (1.5 mm) thick. Cut into 3 to 3 1/2 inch (7.5 to 9 cm) circles. Place 1/2 tbsp. (7 mL) pie filling in center of each. Dampen edges with water. Fold over. Press edges together with floured fork or pinch to seal. Arrange in single layer on tray. Cover until ready to fondue.

Cook pies, a few at a time, in hot (375°F, 190°C) cooking oil in fondue pot, for 2 minutes, turning at halftime to brown other side. Remove with dipping basket or small metal sieve.

Dust pies with icing sugar. Makes 21 pies.

1 pie: 54 Calories; 2.4 g Total Fat; 37 mg Sodium; 1 g Protein; 8 g Carbohydrate; trace Dietary Fiber

Chocolate Doughnut Holes

You may prefer to prepare earlier in the day and use these delectable morsels as a dipper for any of the dessert fondues.

Granulated sugar	1/4 cup	60 mL
Cooking oil	1 tbsp.	15 mL
Egg white (large)	1	1
Milk	1/4 cup	60 mL
Vanilla	1/4 tsp.	1 mL
All-purpose flour	1 1/8 cups	280 mL
Cocoa	4 tsp.	20 mL
Baking powder	1 tsp.	5 mL
Salt	1/8 tsp.	0.5 mL

Cooking oil, for fondue pot (no more
    than 2/3 full)

Granulated sugar, for dusting (optional)
Icing (confectioner's) sugar, for dusting (optional)

Beat sugar, first amount of cooking oil, egg white, milk and vanilla together in medium bowl.

Add flour, cocoa, baking powder and salt. Mix well. Turn out onto lightly floured surface. Roll out to 1/4 inch (6 mm) thick. Cut dough with 1 inch (2.5 cm) cookie cutter. Place on large plate. Cover. Chill for up to 4 hours.

Cook circles, a few at a time, in hot (375°F, 190°C) cooking oil in fondue pot for 2 minutes, turning at halftime to brown other side. Remove with dipping basket or small metal sieve.

Dust with sugar or icing sugar. Makes 32 doughnut holes.

1 doughnut hole: 70 Calories; 5.1 g Total Fat; 24 mg Sodium; 1 g Protein; 5 g Carbohydrate; trace Dietary Fiber

Suggested fondues and dipping sauces: Milky Chocolate Fondue, page 98; Cherry Fondue, page 106; butterscotch, chocolate and lemon sauces.

Quickest Doughnuts

These are not only fast but also fun for the kids to prepare.

Package of refrigerator country-style biscuits (10 biscuits per tube)	12 oz.	340 g
Cooking oil, for fondue pot (no more than 2/3 full)		
Granulated sugar, for dusting (optional)		
Icing (confectioner's) sugar, for dusting (optional)		

Separate biscuits. Cut each biscuit into 4 equal potions. Shape each portion into flat circle. Press your finger through center. Leaving finger in hole, roll dough slightly to prevent hole closing during cooking.

Cook doughnuts, a few at a time, in hot (375°F, 190°C) cooking oil in fondue pot, turning to brown both sides. Remove with dipping basket or small metal sieve.

Dust doughnuts with sugar or icing sugar. Makes 40 doughnuts.

1 doughnut: 79 Calories; 5 g Total Fat; 106 mg Sodium; 1 g Protein; 8 g Carbohydrate; 0 g Dietary Fiber

Best French Toast

For those who like breakfast any time of the day. Try as a dipper for fruit-based dessert fondues.

Baguette, cut into 3/4 inch (2 cm) slices and quartered	1	1
BATTER		
Large eggs	4	4
Milk	1 cup	250 mL
White vinegar	1 tbsp.	15 mL
Granulated sugar (optional)	2 tsp.	10 mL
Salt	1/8 tsp.	0.5 mL
Cooking oil, for fondue pot (no more than 2/3 full)		

(continued on next page)

Pile bread pieces into bowl. Cover until ready to fondue.

Batter: Beat first 5 ingredients together in medium bowl until smooth. Makes 2 cups (500 mL) batter.

Dip bread in batter. Cook in hot 375°F (190°C) cooking oil in fondue pot for about 20 seconds until golden. Makes about 90 pieces.

1 piece: 30 Calories; 1.7 g Total Fat; 38 mg Sodium; 1 g Protein; 3 g Carbohydrate; trace Dietary Fiber

Suggested fondues and dipping sauces: Apricot Fondue, page 104; Lemon Fondue, page 109; maple (or pancake) syrup.

Maple Bud Pastries

Yum! A melted chocolate surprise inside of each cake pastry.

Package of refrigerator country-style biscuits (10 biscuits per tube)	12 oz.	340 g
Maple buds candy	40	40

Cooking oil, for fondue pot (no more than 2/3 full)

Granulated sugar, for dusting (optional)
Icing (confectioner's) sugar, for dusting (optional)

Separate biscuits. Cut each biscuit into 4 equal portions. Shape each portion into flat circle. Place 1 maple bud in center of each portion. Wrap edges around maple bud to form a ball. Pinch to seal.

Cook pastries, a few at a time, in hot (375°F, 190°C) cooking oil in fondue pot for about 2 minutes, turning to brown both sides. Remove with dipping basket or small metal sieve.

Dust pastries with sugar or icing sugar. Makes 40 pastries.

1 pastry: 143 Calories; 2.7 g Total Fat; 109 mg Sodium; 1 g Protein; 30 g Carbohydrate; 0 g Dietary Fiber

Marinades

Marinades are savory liquids that permeate meat, poultry, seafood and vegetables to give added flavor. They work well for any food that is to be cooked in an oil fondue or on a stone grill. Marinating should be done in a non-metal shallow dish, large enough to arrange the food in a single layer. A resealable plastic bag also works well. Thirty minutes is the least amount of time you should marinate meat; twenty-four hours is the best. However, fish generally requires no more than 30 minutes to 4 hours or it will become too soft. Meats that are marinating should be refrigerated. The leftover marinade can be boiled for 5 minutes and used as a basting sauce. Alternatively, it can be served as a dipping sauce if it is brought to a rolling boil for 5 minutes to kill any bacteria from the raw meat.

Marinade For Fish

A marinade that accents fish nicely with soy sauce and sherry flavors.
Use with any firm fish such as swordfish, halibut, snapper and salmon.
Also great for scallops and shrimp.

Soy sauce	1/2 cup	125 mL
Brown sugar, packed	1/4 cup	60 mL
Peanut (or cooking) oil	2 tbsp.	30 mL
Ground ginger	1/2 tsp.	2 mL
Garlic powder	1/2 tsp.	2 mL
Sherry (or alcohol-free sherry)	1/3 cup	75 mL

Combine all 6 ingredients in small bowl. Makes 1 cup (250 mL), enough to marinate 1 1/2 lbs. (680 g) fish.

1 tbsp. (15 mL): 39 Calories; 1.7 g Total Fat; 546 mg Sodium; 1 g Protein; 5 g Carbohydrate; trace Dietary Fiber

Pictured on page 53.

Robust Red Wine Marinade

A light wine flavor with a hint of garlic and ginger that's great for beef.

Dry red wine	1/4 cup	60 mL
Green onion, chopped	1	1
Garlic cloves, minced (or	2	2
1/2 tsp., 2 mL, powder)		
Coarsely chopped gingerroot (or	1 1/2 tsp.	7 mL
1/4 tsp., 1 mL, ground ginger)		
Cooking oil	2 tbsp.	30 mL

Combine all 5 ingredients in small bowl. Makes 1/2 cup (125 mL), enough to marinate 1/2 lb. (225 g) beef.

1 tbsp. (15 mL): 38 Calories; 3.5 g Total Fat; 1 mg Sodium; trace Protein; trace Carbohydrate; trace Dietary Fiber

White Wine Marinade

An extra flavor boost with a strong garlic presence. Use with pork, chicken or seafood.

Dry white wine	1 cup	250 mL
Lemon juice	1 tbsp.	15 mL
Lime juice	1/2 tbsp.	7 mL
Garlic cloves, minced (or 1/2 tsp.,	2	2
2 mL, powder)		
Finely grated gingerroot (or 1/4 tsp.,	1 tsp.	5 mL
1 mL, ground ginger)		
Chopped fresh parsley (or 1 1/2 tsp.,	2 tbsp.	30 mL
7 mL, flakes)		
Salt	1 tsp.	5 mL
Freshly ground pepper	1 tsp.	5 mL

Combine all 8 ingredients in small bowl. Makes 1 cup (250 mL), enough to marinate 1 lb. (454 g) chicken, pork or seafood.

1 tbsp. (15 mL): 11 Calories; 0 g Total Fat; 128 mg Sodium; trace Protein; trace Carbohydrate; trace Dietary Fiber

Pepper Marinade

A very nice teriyaki flavor with a slight bite from the pepper.

Cooking oil	2 tbsp.	30 mL
Soy sauce	2 tbsp.	30 mL
Liquid honey	2 tbsp.	30 mL
Rice vinegar	1 tbsp.	15 mL
Cajun seasoning	1/4 tsp.	1 mL
Freshly ground pepper	1 tsp.	5 mL

Combine all 6 ingredients in small bowl. Makes scant 1/2 cup (125 mL), enough to marinate 1/2 lb. (225 g) chicken.

1 tbsp. (15 mL): 51 Calories; 3.5 g Total Fat; 262 mg Sodium; trace Protein; 5 g Carbohydrate; trace Dietary Fiber

Teriyaki Marinade

Best with beef or chicken strips instead of cubes to maximize flavor.

Soy sauce	1/3 cup	75 mL
Granulated sugar	2 tsp.	10 mL
Finely grated gingerroot (or 1/4 tsp., 1 mL, ground ginger)	1 tsp.	5 mL
Sherry (or alcohol-free sherry)	1/3 cup	75 mL
Garlic clove, minced (or 1/4 tsp., 1 mL, powder)	1	1

Combine all 5 ingredients in small bowl. Makes 2/3 cup (150 mL), enough to marinade 1 1/2 lbs. (680 g) beef or chicken strips.

1 tbsp. (15 mL): 15 Calories; 0 g Total Fat; 520 mg Sodium; 1 g Protein; 2 g Carbohydrate; trace Dietary Fiber

Paré Pointer

New babies rule the household, especially the Prince of Wails.

Ginger Marinade

This may seem like a very small amount of marinade for 1 lb. (454 g) chicken, but it does work. Try it! Then dip in Sesame Sauce, page 69.

Finely chopped gingerroot (or 1/2 tsp., 2 mL, ground ginger)	2 tsp.	10 mL
Brown sugar, packed	1 tbsp.	15 mL
Onion powder	1/4 tsp.	1 mL
Rice wine (sake) or lemon juice	1 tbsp.	15 mL
Orange (or apple) juice	1 tbsp.	15 mL

Combine all 5 ingredients in small bowl. Makes 3 tbsp. (50 mL), enough to marinate 1 lb. (454 g) chicken.

1 tbsp. (15 mL): 25 Calories; 0 g Total Fat; 2 mg Sodium; trace Protein; 5 g Carbohydrate; trace Dietary Fiber

Pictured on page 36.

Beer Marinade

You can actually taste both the beer and the barbecue sauce! Use for beef, chicken or pork.

Beer	3/4 cup	175 mL
Barbecue sauce	1/3 cup	75 mL
Worcestershire sauce	1/2 tsp.	2 mL
Brown sugar, packed	1 1/2 tsp.	7 mL
Dry mustard	1/4 tsp.	1 mL
Cayenne pepper	1/8 tsp.	0.5 mL
Seasoned salt	1/4 tsp.	1 mL
Garlic cloves, slivered (or 1/2 tsp., 2 mL, powder)	2	2

Combine all 8 ingredients in small bowl. Makes 1 1/3 cups (325 mL), enough to marinate 1 1/2 lbs. (680 g) beef, chicken or pork.

1 tbsp. (15 mL): 9 Calories; 0.1 g Total Fat; 48 mg Sodium; trace Protein; 1 g Carbohydrate; trace Dietary Fiber

Fresh Herb And Wine Marinade

Very nice wine flavor and slightly seasoned by the spices. Use with chicken or seafood.

White wine	1/2 cup	125 mL
Chopped fresh tarragon leaves	1 tsp.	5 mL
Chopped fresh thyme leaves	1 tsp.	5 mL
Chopped fresh sweet basil	1 tsp.	5 mL
Lemon juice	1 tsp.	5 mL
Garlic clove, coarsely chopped (or 1/4 tsp., 1 mL, powder)	1	1
Freshly ground pepper, sprinkle		

Combine all 7 ingredients in small bowl. Makes about 1/2 cup (125 mL), enough to marinate 1/2 lb. (225 g) chicken or seafood.

1 tbsp. (15 mL): 12 Calories; 0 g Total Fat; 1 mg Sodium; trace Protein; trace Carbohydrate; trace Dietary Fiber

Pictured on page 144.

Coconut Curry Marinade

A sweet marinade that has a distinctive ginger flavor. Use with chicken.

Coconut milk	1/4 cup	60 mL
Milk	1/4 cup	60 mL
Hot curry paste (available in Asian section of grocery store)	1/2 - 1 tsp.	2 - 5 mL
Granulated sugar	1/2 tsp.	2 mL
Salt	1/2 tsp.	2 mL
Finely chopped gingerroot (or 1/4 tsp., 1 mL, ground ginger)	1 tsp.	5 mL

Combine all 6 ingredients in small bowl. Makes about 1/2 cup (125 mL), enough to marinate 1/2 lb. (225 g) chicken.

1 tbsp. (15 mL): 21 Calories; 1.8 g Total Fat; 153 mg Sodium; trace Protein; 1 g Carbohydrate; trace Dietary Fiber

Dipping Sauces

Variety is the spice of life. Let it be the spice of your next tabletop cooking experience by choosing at least two sauces for dipping meats and vegetables. You can select sweet, savory, creamy and textured sauces to highlight the same meal. Specially designed fondue plates will allow guests to keep each taste sensation separate. As an alternative, give each person several small individual bowls. That way they can double-dip to their heart's content without breaking any etiquette rules!

Cracked Pepper Sauce

Creamy garlic and strong pepper flavors make this a great dipping sauce for beef.

Cream cheese, softened	8 oz.	250 g
Butter (not margarine), softened	1/2 cup	125 mL
Garlic clove, minced (or 1/4 tsp., 1 mL, powder)	1	1
Cracked whole peppercorns	1 tsp.	5 mL
Finely chopped shallots	1 tsp.	5 mL
Salt	1/8 tsp.	0.5 mL
Milk	2 tbsp.	30 mL
Finely chopped pecans	2 tbsp.	30 mL

Beat cream cheese and butter together in small bowl until smooth.

Add garlic, peppercorns, shallots and salt. Beat until well combined. Beat in milk and pecans until well mixed. Serve at room temperature. Makes 1 3/4 cups (425 mL).

1 tbsp. (15 mL): 64 Calories; 6.7 g Total Fat; 70 mg Sodium; 1 g Protein; trace Carbohydrate; trace Dietary Fiber

Pictured on page 36.

Suggested fondues and dipper: Beef Hot Pot, page 11; Basic Beef Fondue, page 20; Mixed Veggies, page 31.

Barbecue Sauce

After tasting this sauce you'll wonder why you ever bought commercial barbecue sauce.

Can of tomato sauce	7 1/2 oz.	213 mL
Brown sugar, packed	3 tbsp.	50 mL
Dry mustard	1 tsp.	5 mL
Apple cider vinegar	1 tbsp.	15 mL
Steak sauce	3 tbsp.	50 mL
Garlic clove, minced (or 1/4 tsp., 1 mL, powder)	1	1
Pepper, sprinkle		

Combine all 7 ingredients in medium saucepan. Heat for about 15 minutes until sugar is dissolved and flavors are blended. Cool. Serve at room temperature. Makes 1 cup (250 mL).

1 tbsp. (15 mL): 17 Calories; 0.1 g Total Fat; 125 mg Sodium; trace Protein; 4 g Carbohydrate; trace Dietary Fiber

Pictured on page 36.

Suggested dippers: Pork Balls, page 16; Meatballs, page 23; Pups In Blankets, page 29.

1. (Vegetable dippers)
2. (Red Snapper with) Marinade For Fish, page 46
3. Lemon Caper Butter, page 66
4. Quick Batter, page 39
5. Rémoulade Sauce, page 59
6. Spicy Cocktail Sauce, page 67

Props Courtesy Of: Linens 'N Things
Stokes

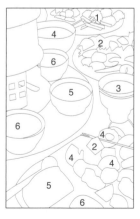

Dipping Sauces

Creamy Mint Sauce

A nice mint taste with a sweet and tangy background. Great with lamb, beef, pork and chicken.

Mint jelly	1/2 cup	125 mL
Light sour cream	1/4 cup	60 mL
Light mayonnaise (or salad dressing)	1/2 cup	125 mL
Finely chopped green onion	2 tbsp.	30 mL
Salt	1/8 tsp.	0.5 mL

Warm mint jelly slightly in small saucepan until liquefied. Cool to room temperature.

Add sour cream, mayonnaise, green onion and salt. Stir until well combined. Chill until ready to fondue. Makes 1 1/3 cups (325 mL).

1 tbsp. (15 mL): 40 Calories; 1.9 g Total Fat; 55 mg Sodium; trace Protein; 6 g Carbohydrate; trace Dietary Fiber

Suggested fondue and dippers: Spinach Dumplings, page 14; Basic Lamb Fondue, page 21; Falafels, page 30.

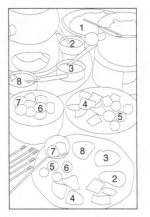

1. (Cooked rice)
2. Cranberry Sauce, page 68
3. Aïoli Sauce, page 56
4. Samosas, page 28
5. Falafels, page 30
6. Pork Balls, page 16
7. Meatballs, page 23
8. Mustard Sauce, page 64

Props Courtesy Of: Stokes

Dipping Sauces

Aïoli Sauce

Wonderful garlic flavor in ay-OH-lee sauce that is good with meat, fish and bread. Will keep for one to two days in the refrigerator. Any unused sauce should be discarded immediately after using.

Garlic cloves, minced (or 1 tsp., 5 mL, powder)	4	4
Salt	1/2 tsp.	2 mL
Egg yolks (large)	4	4
Olive oil	1/2 cup	125 mL
Cooking oil	1/2 cup	125 mL
Lemon juice	2 tsp.	10 mL
White pepper	1/8 tsp.	0.5 mL

Place garlic, salt and egg yolks in blender. Purée until light in color and thickened.

Combine both oils and lemon juice in measuring cup. With machine running, slowly add oil mixture in a thin steady stream through feed tube. Process until thickened to consistency of mayonnaise.

Add white pepper. Stir. Chill until ready to fondue. Makes 1 1/2 cups (375 mL).

1 tbsp. (15 mL): 91 Calories; 10 g Total Fat; 49 mg Sodium; trace Protein; trace Carbohydrate; trace Dietary Fiber

Pictured on page 54.

Suggested dippers: Seasoned Calamari, page 25; boneless, skinless chicken breast cubes; pork tenderloin cubes; sirloin steak cubes; French or Italian bread cubes.

 Fish and seafood do not require a long marinating time as they are naturally tender. Generally, 30 minutes is enough time to transfer the flavors without having the fish fall apart.

Kickin' Hot Sauce

Spicy without being overwhelming.

Can of stewed tomatoes, with juice	14 oz.	398 mL
Small onion, chopped	1	1
Medium green pepper, seeded and chopped	1	1
Jalapeño peppers, seeded and diced (see Note)	2	2
Chopped fresh cilantro	2 tbsp.	30 mL
White vinegar	2 tbsp.	30 mL
Garlic cloves, chopped (or 3/4 tsp., 4 mL, powder)	3	3
Granulated sugar	2 tsp.	10 mL
Hot pepper sauce	1 – 2 tsp.	5 – 10 mL
Salt	1 tsp.	5 mL
Pepper	1/4 tsp.	1 mL

Combine all 11 ingredients in medium saucepan. Bring to a boil. Reduce heat. Simmer, uncovered, for about 30 minutes, stirring occasionally. Process in blender until smooth. Serve at room temperature. Makes 2 cups (500 mL).

1 tbsp. (15 mL): 8 Calories; 0 g Total Fat; 108 mg Sodium; trace Protein; 2 g Carbohydrate; trace Dietary Fiber

Suggested fondue and dipper: Beef Hot Pot, page 11; Fried Cheese, page 32.

Note: Wear gloves when chopping jalapeño peppers and avoid touching your eyes.

 To determine how much meat to prepare for a fondue, allow for a total of 4 oz. (113 g) trimmed meat per person.

Yogurt Cuke Sauce

A good cucumber, garlic and dill combination. Great with beef.

Peeled, grated cucumber, squeezed and blotted dry	1 1/3 cups	325 mL
Plain yogurt	1 cup	250 mL
Chopped fresh dill (or 3/4 tsp, 4 mL, dill weed)	1 tbsp.	15 mL
Lime juice	2 tsp.	10 mL
Garlic clove, minced (or 1/4 tsp., 1 mL, powder)	1	1
Salt	1/4 tsp.	1 mL
Pepper	1/8 tsp.	0.5 mL
Granulated sugar	1 tsp.	5 mL

Combine all 8 ingredients in small bowl. Stir. Chill for 2 to 3 hours to allow flavors to blend. Makes 1 2/3 cups (400 mL).

1 tbsp. (15 mL): 7 Calories; 0.2 g Total Fat; 28 mg Sodium; 1 g Protein; 1 g Carbohydrate; trace Dietary Fiber

Suggested dipper: Falafels, page 30.

Creamy Avocado Dip

Having some tortilla chips close by will ensure this dip disappears quickly.

Ripe avocado, peeled, pitted and mashed	1	1
Light sour cream	2/3 cup	150 mL
Green onion, chopped	1	1
Lemon juice	1 tsp.	5 mL
Garlic clove, minced (or 1/4 tsp., 1 mL, powder)	1	1
Salt	1/2 tsp.	2 mL
Pepper	1/4 tsp.	1 mL
Cayenne pepper (optional)	1/8 tsp.	0.5 mL

(continued on next page)

Combine all 8 ingredients in medium bowl. Stir. Chill for 2 to 3 hours to allow flavors to blend. Makes 1 1/2 cups (375 mL).

1 tbsp. (15 mL): 19 Calories; 1.7 g Total Fat; 51 mg Sodium; trace Protein; 1 g Carbohydrate; trace Dietary Fiber

Suggested dippers: Falafels, page 30; Mixed Veggies, page 31.

Rémoulade Sauce

Creamy mustard and anchovy sauce. Will keep for several days in the refrigerator.

Light mayonnaise (or salad dressing)	1 cup	250 mL
Chopped fresh tarragon leaves (or	1/2 tsp.	2 mL
1/8 tsp., 0.5 mL, dried)		
Capers, drained, rinsed and chopped	1 tbsp.	15 mL
Prepared mustard	1 tsp.	5 mL
Finely chopped gherkins	1 tbsp.	15 mL
Chopped fresh parsley (or 1/2 tsp.,	2 tsp.	10 mL
2 mL, flakes)		
Anchovy paste	1 1/2 tsp.	7 mL
Milk, approximately	1/4 cup	60 mL

Combine first 7 ingredients in small bowl.

Gradually add milk until desired dipping consistency. Chill until ready to fondue. Makes 1 1/3 cups (325 mL).

1 tbsp. (15 mL): 38 Calories; 3.6 g Total Fat; 112 mg Sodium; trace Protein; 1 g Carbohydrate; trace Dietary Fiber

Pictured on page 53.

Suggested dippers: Pork Balls, page 16; Ham Balls, page 19; Meatballs, page 23; assorted fish chunks; seafood.

Paré Pointer

Not everything costs more these days. You can still use a dime as a screwdriver.

Snappy Black Bean Sauce

This sauce is on the salty side due to the black bean sauce.
Especially good with beef.

Garlic cloves, minced (or 1/2 tsp., 2 mL, powder)	2	2
Finely chopped gingerroot (or 1/4 tsp., 1 mL, ground ginger)	1 tsp.	5 mL
Sesame (or cooking) oil	1 tsp.	5 mL
Black bean sauce	2 tbsp.	30 mL
Sherry (or alcohol-free sherry)	2 tbsp.	30 mL
Soy sauce	2 tbsp.	30 mL
Water	1/3 cup	75 mL
Cornstarch	2 tsp.	10 mL
Granulated sugar	1/2 tsp.	2 mL

Sauté garlic and ginger in sesame oil in frying pan for about 30 sconds until softened.

Add black bean sauce, sherry, soy sauce, water, cornstarch and sugar. Stir. Heat and stir until boiling and thickened. Cool to room temperature. Makes 2/3 cup (150 mL).

1 tbsp. (15 mL): 16 Calories; 0.8 g Total Fat; 352 mg Sodium; trace Protein; 2 g Carbohydrate; trace Dietary Fiber

Pictured on page 17.

Suggested fondue: Basic Beef Fondue, page 20.

Orange Sauce

A taste that will remind you of Christmas. Serve with chicken and pork.

Prepared orange juice	1 cup	250 mL
All-purpose flour	1/4 cup	60 mL
Brown sugar, packed	1/4 cup	60 mL
Dry mustard	1/4 tsp.	1 mL
Ground cloves	1 tsp.	5 mL

(continued on next page)

Combine all 5 ingredients in small saucepan. Heat and stir on medium-low until thickened. Cool to room temperature. Makes 1 cup (250 mL).

1 tbsp. (15 mL): 29 Calories; 0.1 g Total Fat; 2 mg Sodium; trace Protein; 7 g Carbohydrate; trace Dietary Fiber

Suggested fondue and dippers: Ham Balls, page 19; Basic Pork Fondue, page 21; Reuben Gems, page 22; Pork And Apple Kabobs, page 136.

Teriyaki Sauce

The traditional teriyaki flavor you were hoping for. So good with chicken and fish.

Garlic clove, minced (or 1/4 tsp., 1 mL, powder)	1	1
Finely chopped gingerroot (or 1/2 tsp., 2 mL, ground ginger)	2 tsp.	10 mL
Sesame (or cooking) oil	2 tsp.	10 mL
Soy sauce	1/4 cup	60 mL
Cold water	1/4 cup	60 mL
Sherry (or alcohol-free sherry) or sake (rice wine)	1/4 cup	60 mL
Brown sugar, packed	1 tbsp.	15 mL
Cornstarch	1 tbsp.	15 mL

Sauté garlic and ginger in sesame oil in small saucepan for about 30 seconds until softened.

Add soy sauce, cold water and sherry. Bring to a boil on medium.

Combine brown sugar and cornstarch in small bowl. Stir into sherry mixture. Heat and stir until boiling, clear and slightly thickened. Serve warm or at room temperature. Makes 2/3 cup (150 mL).

1 tbsp. (15 mL): 24 Calories; 0.8 g Total Fat; 395 mg Sodium; 1 g Protein; 3 g Carbohydrate; trace Dietary Fiber

Suggested dippers: Meatballs, page 23; boneless, skinless chicken breast cubes; assorted fish chunks.

 To determine how many vegetables to serve at a fondue, allow a total of 1/2 lb. (225 g) vegetables per person.

Italian Sauce

Makes a nice dip for meatballs and vegetables with the nice tomato flavor that isn't too tart.

Chopped onion	1/2 cup	125 mL
Garlic clove, minced (or 1/4 tsp., 1 mL, powder)	1	1
Olive (or cooking) oil	1 tbsp.	15 mL
Can of diced tomatoes, with juice	14 oz.	398 mL
Tomato paste	2 tbsp.	30 mL
Dried sweet basil, crushed	2 tsp.	10 mL
Dried whole oregano, crushed	1/4 tsp.	1 mL
Freshly ground pepper, sprinkle		
Grated Parmesan cheese, for garnish		

Sauté onion and garlic in olive oil in frying pan for about 5 minutes until onion is soft and golden.

Add tomatoes with juice, tomato paste, basil, oregano and pepper. Stir. Cover. Heat on low for 30 minutes. Cool slightly. Process in blender until smooth.

Just before serving, sprinkle with Parmesan cheese. Serve warm or at room temperature. Makes 1 1/3 cups (325 mL).

1 tbsp. (15 mL): 12 Calories; 0.7 g Total Fat; 31 mg Sodium; trace Protein; 2 g Carbohydrate; trace Dietary Fiber

Suggested dippers: Spinach Dumplings, page 14; Meatballs, page 23; Mixed Veggies, page 31.

Bacon Blue Cheese Sauce

Great blue cheese flavor that would complement any vegetable.

Sour cream	3/4 cup	175 mL
Blue cheese, finely crumbled (or slightly mashed)	2 oz.	57 g
Lemon juice	1/2 tsp.	2 mL
Chopped green onion	2 tbsp.	30 mL
Real bacon bits	2 tbsp.	30 mL

(continued on next page)

Combine all 5 ingredients in medium bowl. Cover. Chill for 2 to 3 hours to allow flavors to blend. Makes 1 cup (250 mL).

1 tbsp. (15 mL): 27 Calories; 2.2 g Total Fat; 48 mg Sodium; 1 g Protein; trace Carbohydrate; 0 g Dietary Fiber

Suggested dipper and fondue: Tempura Fondue, page 26; Garlic Dipping Squares, page 33.

Niçoise Sauce

A nice blend of tomato, garlic, olive and anchovy flavors. Serve with fresh vegetables or fondue meats and fish.

Small onion, finely chopped	1	1
Garlic cloves, minced (or 1/2 tsp., 2 mL, powder)	2	2
Hard margarine (or butter)	1/4 cup	60 mL
Can of crushed tomatoes	28 oz.	796 mL
Jar of pimiento, drained and finely chopped	2 oz.	57 mL
Finely chopped ripe pitted olives	1/4 cup	60 mL
Granulated sugar	1/4 tsp.	1 mL
Anchovy paste	1/2 tsp.	2 mL
Salt, sprinkle		
Pepper, sprinkle		
Light mayonnaise (or salad dressing)	2 tbsp.	30 mL

Sauté onion and garlic in margarine in large saucepan until soft.

Add tomatoes, pimiento, olives, sugar, anchovy paste, salt and pepper. Stir. Cover. Simmer for 30 minutes. Process with hand blender or in food processor until smooth. Cool.

Stir mayonnaise into tomato mixture. Stir. Chill until ready to fondue. Makes 3 cups (750 mL).

1 tbsp. (15 mL): 15 Calories; 1.3 g Total Fat; 48 mg Sodium; trace Protein; 1 g Carbohydrate; trace Dietary Fiber

Suggested dippers: Fried Cheese, page 32; assorted meat cubes; assorted vegetable chunks.

Mustard Sauce

Be prepared—it's a tangy sauce and great with beef.

Brown sugar, packed	1 cup	250 mL
All-purpose flour	2 tbsp.	30 mL
White vinegar	1/4 cup	60 mL
Water	1/2 cup	125 mL
Prepared mustard	2 tbsp.	30 mL

Combine brown sugar and flour in medium saucepan.

Add vinegar, water and mustard. Heat and stir on medium-low until boiling and thickened. Cool to room temperature. Makes 1 1/3 cups (325 mL).

1 tbsp. (15 mL): 44 Calories; 0.1 g Total Fat; 23 mg Sodium; trace Protein; 11 g Carbohydrate; trace Dietary Fiber

Pictured on page 54 and on page 71.

Suggested fondue and dippers: Beef Dumplings, page 15; Pork Balls, page 16; Ham Balls, page 19; Reuben Gems, page 22; A Snap Fondue, page 24; Pups In Blankets, page 29; Falafels, page 30.

Basil Garlic Mayo

Roasted garlic and fresh basil flavors in a thick creamy sauce. It will become a favorite.

Whole garlic bulb	1	1
Olive (or cooking) oil	1 1/2 tsp.	7 mL
Light mayonnaise (or salad dressing)	1 cup	250 mL
Chopped fresh sweet basil (or 1/2 tsp., 2 mL, dried)	2 tbsp.	30 mL

Remove as much loose skin as possible from outside of garlic bulb. Barely cut top off garlic cloves. Place on foil. Drizzle with olive oil. Wrap tightly. Bake in 350°F (175°C) oven for 35 to 45 minutes until soft. Unwrap. Cool enough to handle. Squeeze pulp from roasted garlic into blender. Discard skin.

Add mayonnaise and basil. Process until smooth. Chill for 2 to 3 hours to allow flavors to blend. Makes 1 cup (250 mL).

(continued on next page)

1 tbsp. (15 mL): 53 Calories; 4.4 g Total Fat; 120 mg Sodium; trace Protein; 3 g Carbohydrate; trace Dietary Fiber

Suggested fondue and dipper: Spinach Dumplings, page 14; Basic Chicken Fondue, page 20.

Madeira Butter Sauce

Wonderful rich flavor with just the right amount of orange.

Sweet Madeira wine	2 tbsp.	30 mL
Chopped green onion	1 tbsp.	15 mL
Whole peppercorns, cracked	4	4
Prepared orange juice	2 tbsp.	30 mL
Egg yolks (large)	3	3
Butter (not margarine), melted and cooled	1 cup	250 mL
Prepared orange juice	2 tbsp.	30 mL
Dried tarragon	1/8 tsp.	0.5 mL
Dried sweet basil	1/8 tsp.	0.5 mL
Ground thyme	1/16 tsp.	0.5 mL
Grated orange peel (optional)	1 tbsp.	15 mL

Combine wine, green onion and peppercorns in small saucepan. Bring to a boil.

Add first amount of orange juice to wine mixture. Stir. Strain into medium heavy saucepan. Discard solids.

Beat egg yolks into wine mixture on low until thickened.

Gradually stir in remaining 6 ingredients. Chill until ready to fondue. Makes 1 cup (250 mL).

1 tbsp. (15 mL): 122 Calories; 13.1 g Total Fat; 125 mg Sodium; 1 g Protein; 1 g Carbohydrate; trace Dietary Fiber

Suggested dipper: Seasoned Calamari, page 25.

Lemon Caper Butter

First you taste the tang of the lemon, then the saltiness of the capers.

Butter (not margarine)	1/2 cup	125 mL
Lemon juice	3 tbsp.	50 mL
Capers, drained and minced	1 tbsp.	15 mL
Parsley flakes	1 tsp.	5 mL

Combine all 4 ingredients in small saucepan. Heat and stir on low until butter is melted. Serve warm. Makes 2/3 cup (150 mL).

1 tbsp. (15 mL): 78 Calories; 8.7 g Total Fat; 103 mg Sodium; trace Protein; trace Carbohydrate; trace Dietary Fiber

Pictured on page 53.

Suggested fondues and dippers: Basic Chicken Fondue, page 20; Seasoned Calamari, page 25; boneless, skinless chicken breast cubes; seafood.

Tartar Sauce

What is fish without tartar sauce?

Light mayonnaise (or salad dressing)	1/2 cup	125 mL
White vinegar	1 tbsp.	15 mL
Sweet pickle relish	1 tbsp.	15 mL
Dry mustard	1/2 tsp.	2 mL
Minced onion	1 tbsp.	15 mL
Salt, sprinkle		
Pepper, sprinkle		

Combine all 7 ingredients in small bowl. Stir. Chill for at least 2 hours to allow flavors to blend. Makes 3/4 cup (175 mL).

1 tbsp. (15 mL): 33 Calories; 3.1 g Total Fat; 76 mg Sodium; trace Protein; 1 g Carbohydrate; trace Dietary Fiber

Pictured on page 35.

Suggested fondues and dippers: Crab Dumplings, page 12; Basic Fish & Seafood Fondue, page 21; A Snap Fondue, page 24.

Dipping Sauces

Dilly-Of-A-Dipping Sauce

The horseradish provides a nice bite.

Light sour cream	1 cup	250 mL
Prepared horseradish	1 tsp.	5 mL
Finely chopped red onion	1 tsp.	5 mL
Chopped fresh dill (or 1/2 tsp., 2 mL, dill weed)	2 tsp.	10 mL
Salt	1/4 tsp.	1 mL
Lemon juice	2 tsp.	10 mL
Granulated sugar	1 tsp.	5 mL

Put all 7 ingredients in small bowl. Stir. Chill for 2 to 3 hours to allow flavors to blend. Makes about 1 cup (250 mL).

1 tbsp. (15 mL): 15 Calories; 1.1 g Total Fat; 44 mg Sodium; trace Protein; 1 g Carbohydrate; trace Dietary Fiber

Suggested fondue and dippers: Tempura Fondue, page 26; Mixed Veggies, page 31; Garlic Dipping Squares, page 33.

Spicy Cocktail Sauce

The strong horseradish flavor with the hint of Worcestershire makes this a great sauce for seafood.

Chili sauce	1/2 cup	125 mL
Ketchup	1/4 cup	60 mL
Prepared horseradish	1 1/2 tsp.	7 mL
Lemon juice	2 tsp.	10 mL
Worcestershire sauce	1 tsp.	5 mL
Salt	1/4 tsp.	1 mL
Granulated sugar	1/4 tsp.	1 mL
Pepper, sprinkle		

Measure all 8 ingredients into small bowl. Stir. Let stand for at least 3 hours to allow flavors to blend. Serve at room temperature. Makes 3/4 cup (175 mL).

1 tbsp. (15 mL): 18 Calories; 0.1 g Total Fat; 267 mg Sodium; trace Protein; 4 g Carbohydrate; 1 g Dietary Fiber

Pictured on page 53.

Suggested fondues and dippers: Crab Dumplings, page 12; Basic Fish & Seafood Fondue, page 21; A Snap Fondue, page 24; seafood.

Dipping Sauces

Plum Sauce

Sweet and sour with a hint of ginger.

Cans of plums (14 oz., 398 mL, each), drained and pitted	2	2
White vinegar	1/4 cup	60 mL
Brown sugar, packed	3/4 cup	175 mL
Ground ginger	1/2 tsp.	2 mL

Process all 4 ingredients in blender or food processor until smooth. Put into medium saucepan. Heat and stir on medium-low until boiling. Remove from heat. Cool to room temperature. Makes 2 cups (500 mL).

1 tbsp. (15 mL): 63 Calories; trace Total Fat; 5 mg Sodium; trace Protein; 17 g Carbohydrate; 1 g Dietary Fiber

Pictured on page 144.

Suggested fondue and dippers: Meatballs, page 23; A Snap Fondue, page 24; boneless, skinless chicken breast cubes; assorted vegetable chunks.

Cranberry Sauce

Wonderful cranberry and orange flavor. Tart with a slight bite from the mustard. Can be served hot or cold.

Cranberry jelly	1/2 cup	125 mL
Grated orange peel	1 tsp.	5 mL
Prepared orange juice	1/4 cup	60 mL
Dry mustard	1/4 tsp.	1 mL
Cornstarch	1 tsp.	5 mL

Place cranberry jelly in heavy saucepan. Heat and stir until melted.

Combine orange peel, orange juice, mustard and cornstarch in small bowl. Stir until cornstarch is dissolved. Add to jelly. Heat and stir until boiling, slightly clear and thickened. Cool to room temperature. Makes 2/3 cup (150 mL).

1 tbsp. (15 mL): 43 Calories; 0.1 g Total Fat; 5 mg Sodium; trace Protein; 11 g Carbohydrate; trace Dietary Fiber

Pictured on page 54.

Suggested dippers: Beef Dumplings, page 15; boneless, skinless chicken (or turkey) breast cubes.

Ginger Sauce

To get the full impact of the ginger flavor, be sure to make ahead of time.

Finely grated gingerroot (or 1/4 tsp., 1 mL, ground ginger)	1 tbsp.	15 mL
Cooking oil	1/4 cup	60 mL
Apple cider vinegar	1/4 cup	60 mL
Soy sauce	1/4 cup	60 mL
Granulated sugar	1 tsp.	5 mL

Combine all 5 ingredients in small bowl. Chill for at least 4 hours or overnight to allow flavors to blend. Stir well before serving. Makes 7/8 cup (200 mL).

1 tbsp. (15 mL): 41 Calories; 4 g Total Fat; 301 mg Sodium; trace Protein; 1 g Carbohydrate; trace Dietary Fiber

Pictured on page 35.

Suggested fondues: Beef Hot Pot, page 11; Basic Pork Fondue, page 21.

Sesame Sauce

A very flavorful sauce with a pleasant little nip. Double for four small dishes.

Light mayonnaise (or salad dressing)	1/4 cup	60 mL
Sesame oil	1 tsp.	5 mL
Sesame seeds	2 tsp.	10 mL
Dried crushed chilies	1/8 tsp.	0.5 mL
Apple juice (or rice wine)	2 tbsp.	30 mL
Chopped green onion	1 tbsp.	15 mL
Sesame seeds	1 tsp.	5 mL

Process first 6 ingredients in blender until almost smooth. Put into small bowl.

Add second amount of sesame seeds. Stir. Chill for 2 to 3 hours to allow flavors to blend. Makes about 1/3 cup (75 mL).

1 tbsp. (15 mL): 55 Calories; 5.2 g Total Fat; 78 mg Sodium; trace Protein; 2 g Carbohydrate; trace Dietary Fiber

Pictured on page 17.

Suggested dippers: Boneless, skinless chicken breast cubes; sirloin steak cubes.

Chutney Curry Sauce

Tangy curry flavor with the added seasoning, sweetness and spice from the chutney.

Light mayonnaise (or salad dressing)	1/2 cup	125 mL
Light cream cheese, softened	4 oz.	125 g
Milk	3 tbsp.	50 mL
Mango chutney, chopped	1/2 cup	125 mL
Medium-hot curry paste (available in Asian section of grocery store)	1 tsp.	5 mL
Lemon juice	2 tsp.	10 mL

Beat mayonnaise, cream cheese and milk together in medium bowl.

Add chutney, curry paste and lemon juice. Beat until well blended. Chill until ready to fondue. Makes 1 1/2 cups (375 mL).

1 tbsp. (15 mL): 32 Calories; 2.5 g Total Fat; 66 mg Sodium; 1 g Protein; 2 g Carbohydrate; trace Dietary Fiber

Pictured on page 18.

Suggested fondue and dippers: Beef Dumplings, page 15; Basic Lamb Fondue, page 21; Fried Cheese, page 32.

1. (Vegetable dippers)
2. Béarnaise Sauce, page 74
3. Mustard Sauce, page 64
4. Pineapple Mango Coleslaw, page 147
5. Basic Oil Fondue, page 20
6. Raisin Honey Sauce, page 73
7. Chili Bread Fingers, page 92

Props Courtesy Of: Anchor Hocking Canada
Winners Stores

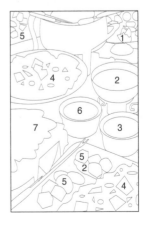

Raisin Honey Sauce

Sweet and slightly spicy. Great with meatballs and chicken.

Dark seedless raisins	1 cup	250 mL
Apple juice	1/2 cup	125 mL
Liquid honey	2 tbsp.	30 mL
Chili sauce	2 tbsp.	30 mL
Soy sauce	1 tbsp.	15 mL
Worcestershire sauce	1 tsp.	5 mL

Process raisins and apple juice in blender or food processor until puréed. Put into small bowl.

Add remaining 4 ingredients. Stir. Serve at room temperature. Makes 1 cup (250 mL).

1 tbsp. (15 mL): 44 Calories; 0.1 g Total Fat; 100 mg Sodium; 1 g Protein; 11 g Carbohydrate; trace Dietary Fiber

Pictured on page 71.

Suggested dippers: Ham Balls, page 19; Meatballs, page 23; boneless, skinless chicken breast cubes.

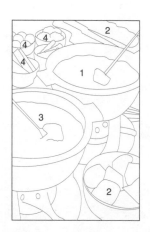

1. Tomato Rarebit Fondue, page 84
2. Pesto Feta Baguette, page 148
3. Seafood Cheese Fondue, page 85
4. (Vegetable dippers)

Props Courtesy Of: Stokes

Béarnaise Sauce

Lovely flavor with a hint of wine, shallots and tarragon.
Discard any unused sauce.

White (or alcohol-free) wine	1/2 cup	125 mL
Dried tarragon, finely crushed	1/2 tsp.	2 mL
Shallots	1 tbsp.	15 mL
Butter (not margarine)	3/4 cup	175 mL
Egg yolks (large)	3	3
Freshly ground pepper, sprinkle		

Heat wine, tarragon and shallots in small saucepan on medium until reduced by half. Cool. Strain into blender.

Heat butter in saucepan to bubbling point but do not brown. Cool.

Add egg yolks and pepper to wine mixture. Process for 3 seconds. With motor running, add butter in a steady steam through hole in lid. Process for about 30 seconds until smooth. Serve warm. Makes 1 cup (250 mL).

1 tbsp. (15 mL): 98 Calories; 10.1 g Total Fat; 95 mg Sodium; 1 g Protein; trace Carbohydrate; trace Dietary Fiber

Pictured on page 71.

Suggested dippers: Boneless, skinless chicken breast cubes; assorted fish chunks; pork tenderloin cubes; sirloin steak cubes.

Paré Pointer

Explaining how her report card marks were so low, Mary said, "Everything gets marked down after Christmas."

Cheese Fondues

While recipes for cheese fondues used to call for exotic cheeses and liberal amounts of wine, we've collected plenty of options that the whole family can enjoy. Good cheeses to use are Emmenthaler, mild Swiss, Cheddar, Edam, Gouda, Gruyère or firm processed cheese. Grated cheese melts quickly over low heat with constant stirring. Heat that is too high will result in a tough, stringy cheese sauce and probably some scorching. If the sauce thickens too much, add a bit of warm wine or butter. If the sauce is too thin, add a bit more cheese or a small amount of cornstarch mixed with wine. If the sauce is lumpy, add a bit of lemon juice or white wine vinegar and stir vigorously until smooth. While you're at it, remind your guests that bread dippers should be swirled right to the bottom of the fondue pot rather than just dipped. This prevents the cheese at the bottom of the pot from being scorched.

Chili Con Queso Fondue

A pretty fondue with a great combination of cheese and tomato, with just enough nip from the green chilies.

Pasteurized cheese loaf (such as Velveeta), cubed (about 4 cups, 1 L)	1 lb.	454 g
Can of tomato sauce	7 1/2 oz.	213 mL
Onion powder	1/4 tsp.	1 mL
Garlic powder	1/4 tsp.	1 mL
Seasoned salt	1/4 tsp.	1 mL
Milk	3 tbsp.	50 mL
Can of diced green chilies, drained and very finely chopped	4 oz.	114 g

Combine first 6 ingredients in large saucepan. Heat and stir on medium until hot and cheese is melted.

Add chilies. Stir to heat through. Carefully pour into fondue pot. Place over low heat. Makes 3 2/3 cups (900 mL).

2 tbsp. (30 mL): 52 Calories; 3.7 g Total Fat; 314 mg Sodium; 3 g Protein; 2 g Carbohydrate; trace Dietary Fiber

Pictured on front cover.

Suggested dippers: Herbed Fondue Bites, page 86; Whole Wheat Focaccia, page 93; assorted bread chips; frozen potato tots, prepared according to package directions; tortilla chips; tortilla wedges, rolled up.

Milky Cheese Fondue

A mild creamy tasting fondue everyone will enjoy.

Cornstarch	1 1/2 tsp.	7 mL
Skim evaporated milk	3/4 cup	175 mL
Light cream cheese, softened and cut up	8 oz.	250 g
Garlic powder	1/4 tsp.	1 mL
Dry mustard	1/8 tsp.	0.5 mL
Seasoned salt	1/8 tsp.	0.5 mL

Stir cornstarch into evaporated milk in medium saucepan until smooth. Heat and stir on medium until boiling and slightly thickened.

Add cream cheese, garlic powder, mustard and seasoned salt. Heat and stir until melted. Carefully pour into fondue pot. Place over low heat. Makes about 1 1/2 cups (375 mL).

2 tbsp. (30 mL): 59 Calories; 3.9 g Total Fat; 170 mg Sodium; 3 g Protein; 3 g Carbohydrate; trace Dietary Fiber

HERBED CHEESE FONDUE: Add 1/4 tsp. (1 mL) dried oregano and/or dried sweet basil.

Suggested dippers: Herbed Fondue Bites, page 86; Handy Biscuit Bites, page 91; Chili Bread Fingers, page 92; Pesto Feta Baguette, page 148; precooked cauliflower and broccoli florets; French, brown, black Russian, pumpernickel or Italian bread cubes.

Parmesan Fondue

The Parmesan cheese flavor is just right, not too overpowering.

Cream cheese, softened and cut up	12 oz.	375 g
Grated Parmesan cheese	1/2 cup	125 mL
Garlic salt	1/4 tsp.	1 mL
Onion powder	1/4 tsp.	1 mL
Milk	1/2 cup	125 mL

(continued on next page)

Cheese Fondues

Combine all 5 ingredients in large saucepan. Beat on low until blended. Heat and stir on low until smooth. Carefully pour into fondue pot. Place over low heat. Makes 2 1/3 cups (575 mL).

2 tbsp. (30 mL): 76 Calories; 7 g Total Fat; 136 mg Sodium; 3 g Protein; 1 g Carbohydrate; 0 g Dietary Fiber

Suggested dippers: Biscuit Bites, page 88; Handy Biscuit Bites, page 91; Tiny Puffs, page 115; warm cooked chicken cubes; wiener chunks; warm cooked cauliflower and broccoli florets; French bread cubes; toast sticks.

Beer Cheese Fondue

A nice blend of cheese and beer flavors.

Grated Swiss cheese	2 cups	500 mL
Grated medium Cheddar cheese	2 cups	500 mL
All-purpose flour	3 tbsp.	50 mL
Dry mustard	1/4 tsp.	1 mL
Chopped chives	2 tsp.	10 mL
Garlic powder	1/8 tsp.	0.5 mL
Pepper	1/8 tsp.	0.5 mL
Ground nutmeg, just a pinch		
Beer	1 cup	250 mL
Worcestershire sauce	1 tsp.	5 mL

Combine first 8 ingredients in large bowl. Toss to coat cheese well. This helps prevent cheese from clumping.

Heat beer and Worcestershire sauce in large saucepan until hot. Add cheese mixture, in 3 or 4 additions, stirring after each addition until melted. Carefully pour into fondue pot. Place over low heat. Makes 2 1/3 cups (575 mL).

2 tbsp. (30 mL): 104 Calories; 7.3 g Total Fat; 111 mg Sodium; 7 g Protein; 2 g Carbohydrate; trace Dietary Fiber

Suggested dippers: Black Russian bread cubes, crumpet chunks, French or Italian bread cubes, rye or pumpernickel bread cubes, spoon-size shredded wheat cereal, warm cooked potato chunks.

Paré Pointer

Pay your taxes with a smile. He tried, but they insisted on money.

Gruyère Fondue

A fresh-tasting fondue with just the right amount of Gruyére cheese and dill.

Grated Gruyère cheese	4 cups	1 L
All-purpose flour	1/4 cup	60 mL
White grape juice	2 cups	500 mL
Garlic clove, minced (or 1/4 tsp., 1 mL, powder)	1	1
Salt	1/2 tsp.	2 mL
Pepper	1/16 tsp.	0.5 mL
Paprika	1/8 tsp.	0.5 mL
Ground nutmeg	1/16 tsp.	0.5 mL
Dill weed	2 tsp.	10 mL

Combine cheese and flour in medium bowl. Toss to coat well.

Heat remaining 7 ingredients in large saucepan, stirring often, until boiling. Add cheese, in 3 or 4 additions, stirring after each addition until melted. Carefully pour into fondue pot. Place over low heat. Serve immediately. Makes about 2 cups (500 mL).

2 tbsp. (30 mL): 129 Calories; 8.4 g Total Fat; 155 mg Sodium; 8 g Protein; 5 g Carbohydrate; trace Dietary Fiber

Suggested dippers: Whole Wheat Focaccia, page 93; cooked scallops; cooked shrimp; assorted cooked vegetable chunks; assorted bread cubes.

Emmenthaler Fondue

Cheesy and garlicky with a hint of nutmeg. Your guests will respond with a resounding, "This tastes great!"

Dry white (or alcohol-free) wine	1 cup	250 mL
Paprika	1/16 tsp.	0.5 mL
Ground nutmeg	1/16 tsp.	0.5 mL
Garlic powder	1/8-1/4 tsp.	0.5-1 mL
Grated Emmenthaler cheese	1 lb.	454 g
All-purpose flour	2 tbsp.	30 mL

(continued on next page)

Cheese Fondues

Heat wine, paprika, nutmeg and garlic powder in medium saucepan.

Toss cheese and flour in medium bowl. Add to wine mixture, in 3 or 4 additions, stirring after each addition until cheese is melted. Heat and stir until boiling and thickened. Carefully pour into fondue pot. Place over low heat. Makes 2 cups (500 mL).

2 tbsp. (30 mL): 116 Calories; 7.5 g Total Fat; 72 mg Sodium; 8 g Protein; 2 g Carbohydrate; trace Dietary Fiber

Suggested dippers: Biscuit Bites, page 88; Whole Wheat Focaccia, page 93; Tiny Puffs, page 115; rolled deli meats; wiener chunks; assorted bread cubes; bagel bites.

Neufchâtel Cheese Fondue

For the authentic taste of Swiss fondue, purchase the cheese from a specialty store that imports European cheeses. This is a great fondue.

Dry white (or alcohol-free) wine	1/2 cup	125 mL
Garlic clove, minced (or 1/4 tsp., 1 mL, powder)	1	1
Grated Gruyère cheese	2 cups	500 mL
Grated Neufchâtel (or Vacherin Fribourgeois or Appenzeller) cheese	2 cups	500 mL
Cornstarch	4 tsp.	20 mL
Kirsch liqueur (optional)	1 tbsp.	15 mL
Ground nutmeg, sprinkle		
Freshly ground pepper, sprinkle		

Combine wine and garlic in fondue pot on medium until boiling.

Combine both cheeses and cornstarch in medium bowl. Toss to coat well. Add to wine mixture, in 3 or 4 additions, stirring after each addition until cheese is melted.

Stir in Kirsch, nutmeg and pepper. Carefully pour into fondue pot. Place over low heat. Makes 2 cups (500 mL).

2 tbsp. (30 mL): 121 Calories; 8.9 g Total Fat; 92 mg Sodium; 8 g Protein; 1 g Carbohydrate; trace Dietary Fiber

Suggested dippers: Assorted vegetable chunks; assorted bread cubes.

Blue Cheese Fondue

Pungent and colorful. For those old cheese fans.

Milk	1 cup	250 mL
Cornstarch	1 tbsp.	15 mL
Grated medium Cheddar cheese	1 cup	250 mL
Cream cheese, softened and cut up	8 oz.	250 g
Blue cheese, cut up	5 oz.	140 g
Garlic powder	1/4 tsp.	1 mL
Onion powder	1/4 tsp.	1 mL
Salt	1/4 tsp.	1 mL

Stir milk into cornstarch in large saucepan until smooth. Heat and stir on medium until boiling and thickened. Reduce heat.

Add Cheddar cheese. Beat until smooth.

Add cream cheese, blue cheese, garlic powder, onion powder and salt. Beat until smooth. Carefully pour into fondue pot. Place over low heat. Makes 2 1/4 cups (550 mL).

2 tbsp. (30 mL): 103 Calories; 8.8 g Total Fat; 210 mg Sodium; 4 g Protein; 2 g Carbohydrate; trace Dietary Fiber

Suggested dippers: Garlic sausage cubes, ham cubes, assorted vegetable chunks, French bread cubes, fried potato nuggets.

Sharp Cheddar Cheese Fondue

Strong Cheddar flavor in a creamy texture.

Milk	1 1/2 cups	375 mL
All-purpose flour	3 tbsp.	50 mL
Grated sharp Cheddar cheese	1 1/2 cups	375 mL
Freshly ground pepper, sprinkle		

Stir milk into flour in saucepan until smooth. Heat and stir on medium until starting to simmer and thicken.

Add cheese and pepper. Heat and stir until cheese is melted. Carefully pour into fondue pot. Place over low heat. Makes 2 cups (500 mL).

(continued on next page)

2 tbsp. (30 mL): 58 Calories; 3.8 g Total Fat; 78 mg Sodium; 4 g Protein; 2 g Carbohydrate; trace Dietary Fiber

Suggested dippers: Chili Bread Fingers, page 92; assorted cooked vegetable chunks; assorted bread cubes.

Tomato Soup Cheese Fondue

Make sure your dippers are unsalted and a bit bland as the soup and cheese offer all the saltiness you will need.

Can of condensed tomato soup	10 oz.	284 mL
Grated medium Cheddar cheese	2 cups	500 mL
Prepared mustard	1 tsp.	5 mL
Paprika	1/4 tsp.	1 mL
Pepper	1/16 tsp.	0.5 mL
Chopped chives	1 tsp.	5 mL
Parsley flakes	1 tsp.	5 mL
Dried sweet basil	1/8 tsp.	0.5 mL
Dried whole oregano	1/8 tsp.	0.5 mL
Ground nutmeg	1/16 tsp.	0.5 mL

Combine all 10 ingredients in large saucepan. Heat and stir on medium until smooth. Carefully pour into fondue pot. Place over low heat. Makes 1 1/3 cups (325 mL).

2 tbsp. (30 mL): 106 Calories; 7.6 g Total Fat; 329 mg Sodium; 6 g Protein; 4 g Carbohydrate; trace Dietary Fiber

Suggested dippers: Biscuit Bites, page 88; Handy Biscuit Bites, page 91; Tiny Puffs, page 115; Pesto Feta Baguette, page 148; French or Italian bread cubes; toast fingers; toasted English muffin chunks.

Paré Pointer

After eating the book last week and the reel of film this week, the goat told a friend goat that he thought the book was better.

Pizza Fondue

Pizza by the bite—soft and rich.

Lean ground beef	1/2 lb.	225 g
Finely chopped onion	1/2 cup	125 mL
Cooking oil	1 tsp.	5 mL
Can of pizza sauce	14 oz.	398 mL
Pepper	1/16 tsp.	0.5 mL
Dried whole oregano	1/2 tsp.	2 mL
Dried sweet basil	1/2 tsp.	2 mL
Grated part-skim mozzarella cheese	2 cups	500 mL
Grated medium Cheddar cheese	1 cup	250 mL
Grated Parmesan cheese	1/4 cup	60 mL

Scramble-fry ground beef and onion in cooking oil in large saucepan until beef is no longer pink. Drain.

Add remaining 7 ingredients. Heat and stir until cheese is melted. Carefully pour into fondue pot. Place over low heat. Makes 3 1/2 cups (875 mL).

2 tbsp. (30 mL): 64 Calories; 4 g Total Fat; 166 mg Sodium; 5 g Protein; 2 g Carbohydrate; trace Dietary Fiber

Pictured on page 90.

Suggested dippers: Herbed Fondue Bites, page 86; Biscuit Bites, page 88; pepperoni slices; salami chunks; green and red pepper chunks; mushrooms; tiny cooked new potatoes or canned potato cubes; Italian and French bread cubes; toasted English muffin chunks.

 Chill any leftover cheese fondue. Warm in small saucepan on low until smooth. Use on toast, baked potatoes, cauliflower or tortilla chips. Also add to soups as a great flavor booster at end of cooking time. Do not bring soup to a boil after adding cheese to prevent curdling.

Broccoli Cheese Fondue

Very cheesy with a strong broccoli presence. The garlic nip is an added bonus.

Frozen chopped broccoli (about 10 oz., 285 g)	2 cups	500 mL
Water		
Can of condensed cream of mushroom soup	10 oz.	284 mL
Pasteurized cheese loaf (such as Velveeta), cubed (about 4 cups, 1 L)	1 lb.	454 g
Garlic powder	1/2 tsp.	2 mL
Hot pepper sauce	1/8 tsp.	0.5 mL

Cook broccoli in water in large saucepan for about 7 minutes until tender. Drain. Chop very fine. Return to saucepan.

Add soup, cheese, garlic powder and hot pepper sauce. Heat on medium-low, stirring often, until hot and cheese is melted. Carefully pour into fondue pot. Place over low heat. Makes 4 1/2 cups (1.1 L).

2 tbsp. (30 mL): 57 Calories; 4.4 g Total Fat; 241 mg Sodium; 3 g Protein; 1 g Carbohydrate; trace Dietary Fiber

Pictured on page 89.

Suggested dippers: Biscuit Bites, page 88; warm wiener chunks; warm cooked vegetable chunks; assorted bread cubes; corn chips.

Paré Pointer

It's best to borrow from a pessimist.
He might not expect you to pay him back.

Tomato Rarebit Fondue

This cheese, tomato, Dijon mustard and Worcestershire medley is delightful.

Hard margarine (or butter)	2 tbsp.	30 mL
All-purpose flour	2 tbsp.	30 mL
Milk	1 cup	250 mL
Can of tomato paste	5 1/2 oz.	156 mL
Dijon mustard	1 tsp.	5 mL
Worcestershire sauce	1 tbsp.	15 mL
Onion powder	1/4 tsp.	1 mL
Granulated sugar	1 tsp.	5 mL
Dried sweet basil	1/8 tsp.	0.5 mL
Pepper	1/16 tsp.	0.5 mL
Grated sharp Cheddar cheese	2 cups	500 mL

Melt margarine in large saucepan. Mix in flour until smooth. Gradually stir in milk. Heat and stir on medium until boiling and thickened. Reduce heat to low.

Add next 7 ingredients. Stir.

Add cheese. Stir until melted. Carefully pour into fondue pot. Place over low heat. Makes 2 cups (500 mL).

2 tbsp. (30 mL): 90 Calories; 6.4 g Total Fat; 135 mg Sodium; 5 g Protein; 4 g Carbohydrate; trace Dietary Fiber

Pictured on page 72.

Suggested dippers: Biscuit Bites, page 88; Chili Bread Fingers, page 92; Whole Wheat Focaccia, page 93; crumpet chunks; toasted English muffin chunks; French and Italian bread cubes; toast fingers.

Paré Pointer
Since there is safety in numbers, always carry a math book.

Seafood Cheese Fondue

Creamy cheese and seafood flavor.

Boston bluefish fillets	14 oz.	395 g
Boiling water, to cover		
Salt	1/4 tsp.	1 mL
Milk	1 cup	250 mL
Cream cheese, softened and cut up	8 oz.	250 g
Grated medium Cheddar cheese	1 cup	250 mL
Onion powder	1/2 tsp.	2 mL
Chopped chives	1 tsp.	5 mL
Can of crabmeat, drained, cartilage removed, flaked	4 1/4 oz.	120 g

Cook fish in boiling water and salt until fish flakes easily when tested with a fork. Drain. Cool. Shred with fork. Set aside.

Combine next 5 ingredients in large saucepan. Heat and stir on medium until cheese is melted.

Add fish and crab. Stir to heat through. Carefully pour into fondue pot. Place over low heat. Makes 3 1/2 cups (875 mL).

2 tbsp. (30 mL): 70 Calories; 5 g Total Fat; 90 mg Sodium; 5 g Protein; 1 g Carbohydrate; 0 g Dietary Fiber

Pictured on page 72.

Suggested dippers: Crackers, toasted English muffin chunks, French bread cubes, melba toast.

Paré Pointer

A burglar fell into the cement mixture. He is now a hardened criminal.

Herbed Fondue Bites

The rosemary and oregano make this great to serve warm
with any of the cheese and sauce fondues in this book.

Milk	1 cup	250 mL
Hard margarine (or butter)	3 tbsp.	50 mL
All-purpose flour	1 1/2 cups	375 mL
Instant yeast	2 1/2 tsp.	12 mL
Granulated sugar	2 1/2 tsp.	12 mL
Salt	1/2 tsp.	2 mL
Dried rosemary, lightly crushed	1/2 tsp.	2 mL
Dried thyme	1/2 tsp.	2 mL
Dried whole oregano	1/2 tsp.	2 mL
All-purpose flour, approximately	1 1/2 cups	375 mL

Heat milk in small saucepan on low until hot, but not boiling. Add margarine. Heat and stir until margarine is melted.

Combine first amount flour, yeast, sugar, salt, rosemary, thyme and oregano in medium bowl. Add milk mixture. Beat for 2 minutes.

Work in enough of second amount of flour until dough pulls away from sides of bowl. Turn out onto lightly floured surface. Knead for about 5 minutes until dough is smooth and elastic. Place dough in greased bowl, turning once to grease top. Cover with tea towel. Let stand in oven with light on and door closed for about 45 minutes until doubled in bulk. Punch dough down. Shape into loaf. Place in greased 9 × 5 × 3 inch (22 × 12.5 × 7.5 cm) loaf pan. Cover with tea towel. Let stand in oven with light on and door closed for about 45 minutes until doubled in size. Bake in 350°F (175°C) oven for about 40 minutes until well browned and hollow-sounding when tapped. Turn out onto wire rack to cool. Break or cut into bite-sized pieces. Place on lightly greased baking sheet. Bake in 350°F (175°C) oven for about 8 minutes until lightly browned. Makes 1 loaf. Cuts into about 70 pieces.

1 piece: 28 Calories; 0.6 g Total Fat; 25 mg Sodium; 1 g Protein; 5 g Carbohydrate; trace Dietary Fiber

Pictured on page 89.

Suggested fondues: Chili Con Queso Fondue, page 75; Milky Cheese Fondue, page 76; Pizza Fondue, page 82.

(continued on next page)

HERBED FONDUE BREAD STICKS: Cut dough into 32 equal portions. Roll out on damp surface to 7 inch (18 cm) ropes. Cover with tea towel. Let rise for 20 minutes. Bake in 350°F (175°C) oven for 15 minutes until lightly browned.

Pictured on front cover.

Shrimp Cheese Fondue

A shrimp fondue is easy yet seems so elegant.

Cans of broken shrimp (4 oz., 113 g, each), with liquid	2	2
Mayonnaise (or salad dressing)	1/4 cup	60 mL
Grated Monterey Jack cheese	2 cups	500 mL
Lemon juice	1 tbsp.	15 mL
Onion powder	1/4 tsp.	1 mL
Garlic powder	1/8 tsp.	0.5 mL

Process shrimp with liquid and mayonnaise in blender until quite smooth. Pour into medium saucepan.

Add cheese, lemon juice, onion powder and garlic powder. Heat and stir until cheese is melted. Carefully pour into fondue pot. Place over low heat. Makes 2 1/4 cups (550 mL).

2 tbsp. (30 mL): 85 Calories; 6.6 g Total Fat; 105 mg Sodium; 6 g Protein; trace Carbohydrate; 0 g Dietary Fiber

Suggested dippers: Biscuit Bites, page 88; frozen potato tots, prepared according to package directions; pumpernickel and dark rye bread cubes; toast fingers.

Paré Pointer
When she first heard about the Dead Sea she was surprised.
She didn't even know it was sick.

Biscuit Bites

These soft and airy miniature biscuits can be speared with a fondue fork and dipped without falling apart.

All-purpose flour	1 cup	250 mL
Granulated sugar	2 tsp.	10 mL
Baking powder	1 3/4 tsp.	9 mL
Salt	1/4 tsp.	1 mL
Hard margarine (or butter)	1/4 cup	60 mL
Milk, approximately	1/2 cup	125 mL

Combine flour, sugar, baking powder and salt in medium bowl. Cut in margarine until crumbly.

Stir in enough milk to form a sticky batter. Drop by teaspoonfuls onto greased baking sheet. Bake in 425°F (220°C) oven for about 8 minutes until golden. Makes 28 biscuit bites.

1 biscuit bite: 36 Calories; 1.8 g Total Fat; 67 mg Sodium; 1 g Protein; 4 g Carbohydrate; trace Dietary Fiber

Suggested fondues: Parmesan Fondue, page 76; Emmenthaler Fondue, page 78; Tomato Soup Cheese Fondue, page 81; Pizza Fondue, page 82; Broccoli Cheese Fondue, page 83; Tomato Rarebit Fondue, page 84; Shrimp Cheese Fondue, page 87; Chocolate Solo Fondue, page 101; Bumbleberry Fondue, page 105; Marmalade Fondue, page 111; Black Currant Fondue, page 112.

1. Broccoli Cheese Fondue, page 83
2. (Vegetable dippers)
3. Ham Balls, page 19
4. Handy Biscuit Bites, page 91
5. Herbed Fondue Bites, page 86

Props Courtesy Of: Cherison Enterprises Inc.
                     Dansk Gifts

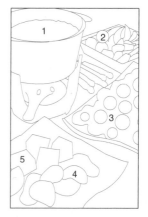

Handy Biscuit Bites

There is no easier way than this to provide warm biscuits at your next cheese fondue.

Package of refrigerator country-style biscuits (10 biscuits per tube)	12 oz.	340 g

Cut each biscuit into 8 equal wedges. Arrange in single layer on greased baking sheet. Bake in 400°F (205°C) oven for about 10 minutes until golden. Makes 80 biscuit bites.

1 biscuit bite: 11 Calories; 0.2 g Total Fat; 53 mg Sodium; trace Protein; 2 g Carbohydrate; 0 g Dietary Fiber

Pictured on page 89.

Suggested fondues: Milky Cheese Fondue, page 76; Parmesan Fondue, page 76; Tomato Soup Cheese Fondue, page 81.

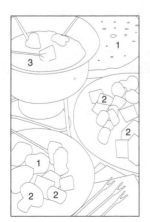

1. Whole Wheat Focaccia, page 93
2. (Vegetable and fruit dippers, and wiener chunks)
3. Pizza Fondue, page 82

Props Courtesy Of: The Bay

Chili Bread Fingers

Soft and chewy with a mild chili flavor, a welcome addition to cheese and sauce fondues.

All-purpose flour	1 7/8 cups	450 mL
Granulated sugar	1/4 cup	60 mL
Salt	1 1/2 tsp.	7 mL
Instant yeast	2 1/2 tsp.	12 mL
Water	3/4 cup	175 mL
Hard margarine (or butter)	1 1/2 tbsp.	25 mL
Large egg (room temperature)	1	1
Chili powder	2 tsp.	10 mL
All-purpose flour, approximately	1 cup	250 mL
Large egg, fork-beaten	1	1
Poppy seeds	1 tsp.	5 mL

Combine first amount of flour, sugar, salt and yeast in large bowl. Mix thoroughly.

Heat water and margarine in small saucepan on medium-low until margarine is melted and quite warm. Gradually add to flour mixture. Beat on medium for about 2 minutes, scraping down sides as necessary.

Beat in first egg and chili powder. Stir in enough of second amount of flour until dough pulls away from sides of bowl. Turn out onto lightly floured surface. Knead for about 5 minutes until dough is smooth and elastic. Place dough in greased bowl, turning once to grease top. Cover with tea towel. Let stand in oven with light on and door closed for 1 hour until doubled in bulk. Punch dough down. Turn out onto lightly floured surface. Divide dough into 4 equal portions. Divide each portion into 4 equal portions. Roll each portion into 7 inch (18 cm) rope. Twist slightly. Place on greased baking sheet. Cover. Let rise in oven with light on and door closed for 30 minutes.

Brush each bread stick with second egg. Sprinkle with poppy seeds. Bake in 375°F (190°C) oven for about 20 minutes until golden. Transfer to wire rack to cool. Makes 16 bread sticks.

1 bread stick: 119 Calories; 2.2 g Total Fat; 249 mg Sodium; 3 g Protein; 21 g Carbohydrate; 1 g Dietary Fiber

Pictured on page 71.

Suggested fondues: Milky Cheese Fondue, page 76; Sharp Cheddar Cheese Fondue, page 80; Tomato Rarebit Fondue, page 84; Appetizer Fondue, page 95.

Whole Wheat Focaccia

You may want to serve individual cheese and sauce fondues with
these hearty tasting wedges. Then there will be guilt-free double dipping.

Granulated sugar	1 tsp.	5 mL
Warm water	1/4 cup	60 mL
Active dry yeast	2 1/2 tsp.	12 mL
All-purpose flour	2 1/2 cups	625 mL
Whole wheat flour	1 cup	250 mL
Flaxseed	2 tbsp.	30 mL
Salt	1 tsp.	5 mL
Olive oil	2 tsp.	10 mL
Water	1 cup	250 mL
Olive oil	1 tbsp.	15 mL
Fresh rosemary leaves (or 1/4 tsp., 1 mL, dried)	1 tsp.	5 mL

Combine sugar and warm water in small bowl. Sprinkle yeast over top. Let stand for 10 minutes. Stir to dissolve yeast.

Combine both flours, flaxseed and salt in large bowl. Make a well in center. Add yeast mixture to well.

Add first amount of olive oil and second amount water to well. Stir until mixed. Turn out onto lightly floured surface. Knead for 8 to 10 minutes until dough is smooth and elastic. Place dough in greased bowl, turning once to grease top. Cover with tea towel. Let stand in oven with light on and door closed for 1 hour until doubled in bulk. Punch down dough. Roll out and press in greased 12 inch (30 cm) pizza pan. Make dents in top of loaf with pointy end of wooden spoon or fingertips.

Drizzle second amount of olive oil over top. Sprinkle with rosemary. Bake in 400°F (205°C) oven for about 25 minutes until golden. Cuts into 16 wedges.

1 wedge: 123 Calories; 2.2 g Total Fat; 150 mg Sodium; 4 g Protein; 22 g Carbohydrate; 2 g Dietary Fiber

Pictured on page 90.

Suggested fondues: Chili Con Queso Fondue, page 75; Gruyère Fondue, page 78; Emmenthaler Fondue, page 78; Tomato Rarebit Fondue, page 84.

Sauce Fondues

Sometimes a fondue defies any easy description. The recipes in this section are not oil or broth cooking liquids and don't have cheese as a main ingredient, nor are they dessert fondues. Regardless, they are delicious for a main meal or appetizer. If you have (or can borrow) more than one fondue pot, pair one of these sauce fondues with a traditional oil fondue, and allow guests to cook their meat in the oil before dipping it into a second heated sauce.

Sweet And Sour Fondue

A little different than the usual fondue but try it, you'll like it.

Water	2 cups	500 mL
Cornstarch	2 tbsp.	30 mL
Soy sauce	2 1/2 tbsp.	37 mL
White vinegar	2 tbsp.	30 mL
Brown sugar, packed	1/4 cup	60 mL
Ketchup	3 tbsp.	50 mL
Chicken bouillon powder	2 tsp.	10 mL

Stir water into cornstarch in medium saucepan until smooth.

Add remaining 5 ingredients. Heat and stir for about 5 minutes until boiling and thickened. Carefully pour into fondue pot. Place over low heat. Makes 2 cups (500 mL).

2 tbsp. (30 mL): 14 Calories; 0.1 g Total Fat; 268 mg Sodium; trace Protein; 3 g Carbohydrate; trace Dietary Fiber

Suggested dippers: Cooked Crab Dumplings, page 12; cooked Pork Balls, page 16; cooked Meatballs, page 23; cooked Pups In Blankets, page 29; cooked fish finger sticks, cut into chunks; ham cubes; wiener chunks; cheese chunks.

Appetizer Fondue

A great way to warm up the taste buds.

Can of tomatoes, with juice	14 oz.	398 mL
Can of tomato sauce	7 1/2 oz.	213 mL
Envelope of spaghetti sauce mix	1 1/2 oz.	43 g
Brown sugar, packed	1 tsp.	5 mL
Garlic salt	1/4 tsp.	1 mL
Pepper	1/4 tsp.	1 mL
Water	2 tbsp.	30 mL
Cornstarch	2 tbsp.	30 mL
Grated part-skim mozzarella cheese	2 tbsp.	30 mL

Process tomatoes with juice in blender until smooth. Pour into large saucepan.

Add tomato sauce, spaghetti sauce mix, brown sugar, garlic salt and pepper. Bring to a boil, stirring often.

Stir water into cornstarch in small cup until smooth. Gradually stir into tomato mixture. Heat and stir until boiling and thickened.

Add cheese. Heat and stir until melted. Carefully pour into fondue pot. Place over low heat. Makes 2 3/4 cups (675 mL).

2 tbsp. (30 mL): 17 Calories; 0.2 g Total Fat; 263 mg Sodium; 1 g Protein; 4 g Carbohydrate; trace Dietary Fiber

Suggested dippers: Cooked Meatballs, page 23; Chili Bread Fingers, page 92; brown-and-serve sausage chunks; cocktail wieners, whole or halved, or regular wiener chunks; cooked shrimp; garlic and summer sausage cubes.

Paré Pointer

The sparrows flew into the library looking for bookworms.

Beer Fondue

Have your pizza and beer in a pot.

Can of pizza sauce	14 oz.	398 mL
Liquid smoke	1/2 tsp.	2 mL
Worcestershire sauce	2 tsp.	10 mL
Brown sugar, packed	2 1/2 tbsp.	37 mL
Beer	1 cup	250 mL
Salt	1/8 tsp.	0.5 mL
Water	3 tbsp.	50 mL
Cornstarch	2 tbsp.	30 mL

Combine pizza sauce, liquid smoke, Worcestershire sauce, brown sugar, beer and salt in large saucepan. Bring to a boil on medium, stirring often.

Stir water into cornstarch in small cup until smooth. Gradually stir into beer mixture. Heat and stir until boiling and thickened. Carefully pour into fondue pot. Place over low heat. Makes 2 3/4 cups (675 mL).

2 tbsp. (30 mL): 21 Calories; 0.1 g Total Fat; 118 mg Sodium; trace Protein; 4 g Carbohydrate; trace Dietary Fiber

Suggested dippers: Cooked Meatballs, page 23; wiener chunks; French bread cubes.

Creamy Curry Fondue

Have the taste without the heat. Mild and full-bodied.

Can of condensed cream of chicken soup	10 oz.	284 mL
Milk	1/4 cup	60 mL
Curry powder	1 tsp.	5 mL
Chopped chives	2 tsp.	10 mL

Combine soup and milk in medium saucepan. Stir vigorously until mixed.

(continued on next page)

Add curry powder and chives. Heat, stirring often, until hot and smooth. Carefully pour into fondue pot. Place over low heat. Makes 1 1/3 cups (325 mL).

2 tbsp. (30 mL): 28 Calories; 1.7 g Total Fat; 216 mg Sodium; 1 g Protein; 2 g Carbohydrate; trace Dietary Fiber

Suggested dippers: Cooked Meatballs, page 23; ham cubes; wiener chunks; warm cooked cauliflower florets; assorted bread cubes.

Bangers And Beans Fondue

A twist to an old favorite in Britain. Can be served with toast!

Bacon slices, diced	2	2
Can of beans in tomato sauce, puréed	14 oz.	398 mL
Fancy (mild) molasses	1 tbsp.	15 mL
Ketchup	1/4 cup	60 mL
Worcestershire sauce	2 tsp.	10 mL
Dry mustard	1/4 tsp.	1 mL

Fry bacon in large saucepan until cooked but not crisp.

Add beans, stirring to absorb bacon drippings.

Add remaining 4 ingredients. Heat and stir on medium until hot. Carefully pour into fondue pot. Place over low heat. Makes 1 2/3 cups (400 mL).

2 tbsp. (30 mL): 53 Calories; 1.6 g Total Fat; 206 mg Sodium; 2 g Protein; 9 g Carbohydrate; 2 g Dietary Fiber

Suggested dippers: Cooked large sausages, cut into cubes or coins; toast triangles.

Paré Pointer

His report on milk was short because he wrote about condensed milk.

Dessert Fondues

Chocolate fondues were introduced in New York in 1966 and quickly became a hit, increasing the popularity of all fondues. Fruit-based fondues are as welcome an end to the meal as are chocolate fondues. Also included in this section are a variety of dippers to complement both. Remember to towel dry any fruit. That way the sauce will remain free of water and will cling better to the fruit. In the case of a chocolate fondue or sauce, water droplets may cause the sauce to seize.

Milky Chocolate Fondue

*The sour cream cuts some of the sweetness and makes for
a very pretty presentation.*

Evaporated milk	2/3 cup	150 mL
Semisweet chocolate chips	1 cup	250 mL
Large marshmallows, cut up	15	15
(or 2 1/2 cups, 625 mL, miniature)		
Sour cream	1 1/2 tbsp.	25 mL
Evaporated milk (or sour cream)	1 tbsp.	15 mL

Combine first 3 ingredients in medium saucepan. Heat on medium-low, stirring often, until smooth. Carefully pour into fondue pot. Place over low heat.

Combine sour cream and evaporated milk in small cup. Drop dabs onto chocolate mixture. Swirl with knife through chocolate mixture. Makes 1 3/4 cups (425 mL).

2 tbsp. (30 mL): 102 Calories; 4.9 g Total Fat; 20 mg Sodium; 2 g Protein; 15 g Carbohydrate; 1 g Dietary Fiber

Pictured on page 125 and on back cover.

Suggested dippers: Chocolate Doughnut Holes, page 43; Ladyfingers, page 116; Peanut Butter Cookies, page 117; apple wedges; banana and pear chunks; chocolate cake chunks; pound cake fingers; tiny cream puffs.

Raspberry Chocolate Fondue

Because this is a thick fondue, more chocolate will stick to the dipper.

Frozen raspberries in syrup, thawed	15 oz.	425 g
Miniature marshmallows	2 cups	500 mL
Unsweetened chocolate baking squares (1 oz., 28 g, each), cut up	4	4

Process raspberries with syrup in blender until almost smooth. Strain into heavy medium saucepan. Discard solids. Bring to a simmer on medium.

Add marshmallows. Heat and stir on low until melted.

Add chocolate. Heat and stir until melted. Carefully pour into fondue pot. Place over low heat. Makes 2 cups (500 mL).

2 tbsp. (30 mL): 80 Calories; 3.8 g Total Fat; 4 mg Sodium; 1 g Protein; 13 g Carbohydrate; 2 g Dietary Fiber

Suggested dippers: Macaroons, page 113; Chocolate Bites, page 118; Popcorn Clusters, page 118; cake chunks; marshmallows.

 Choose firm fruit for dipping. Delicate fruit, such as watermelon or raspberries, may not stay on the fork and get lost in the fondue pot.

Mocha Cherry Fondue

Yummy chocolate and coffee flavor with a mild cherry presence.

Semisweet chocolate baking squares (1 oz., 28 g, each), cut up	8	8
Whipping cream	1 cup	250 mL
Kirsch liqueur (or 1/2 tsp., 2 mL, cherry flavoring)	3 tbsp.	50 mL
Instant coffee granules	1 tbsp.	15 mL

Combine all 4 ingredients in large heavy saucepan. Heat and stir on medium-low until smooth. Carefully pour into fondue pot. Place over low heat. Makes 2 cups (500 mL).

2 tbsp. (30 mL): 117 Calories; 8.9 g Total Fat; 7 mg Sodium; 1 g Protein; 9 g Carbohydrate; 1 g Dietary Fiber

Suggested dippers: Mini-Cakes, page 112; Tiny Puffs, page 115; apple wedges; banana chunks; canned pineapple chunks, well drained; pitted cherries; strawberries; cake chunks.

Brandied Mocha Fondue

Smooth chocolate and cinnamon flavor with a hint of brandy.

Milk chocolate chips	2 cups	500 mL
Skim evaporated milk	7 tbsp.	115 mL
Instant coffee granules	1 tbsp.	15 mL
Brandy flavoring	1 tsp.	5 mL
Ground cinnamon	1/8 tsp.	0.5 mL

Combine all 5 ingredients in heavy medium saucepan. Heat and stir on medium-low until smooth. Carefully pour into fondue pot. Place over low heat. Makes 1 cup (250 mL).

2 tbsp. (30 mL): 231 Calories; 13.1 g Total Fat; 51 mg Sodium; 4 g Protein; 27 g Carbohydrate; 1 g Dietary Fiber

Suggested dippers: Tiny Puffs, page 115; Ladyfingers, page 116; Chocolate Bites, page 118; assorted fruit chunks; cake chunks.

Chocolate Solo Fondue

Rich chocolate flavor that can only be described as decadent.

Semisweet chocolate chips	2 cups	500 mL
Half-and-half (or whipping) cream	1/2 cup	125 mL

Heat chocolate chips and cream in heavy medium saucepan on medium-low, stirring often, until smooth. Carefully pour into fondue pot. Place over low heat. Makes 1 1/2 cups. (375 mL).

2 tbsp. (30 mL): 142 Calories; 9 g Total Fat; 5 mg Sodium; 1 g Protein; 18 g Carbohydrate; 2 g Dietary Fiber

CHOCOLATE MINT FONDUE: Omit semisweet chocolate chips. Add same amount of chocolate mint chips.

Suggested dippers: Biscuit Bites, page 88; Peanut Butter Cookies, page 117; assorted fruit chunks; cake chunks; cookie pieces.

Paré Pointer

Knock, knock. Who's there? Francis. Francis who?
Francis a country in Europe.

Peachy White Chocolate Fondue

Sweet white chocolate and pleasant peach flavor.

Half-and-half cream	1/4 cup	60 mL
Peach drink crystals	1 tbsp.	15 mL
White chocolate baking squares (1 oz., 28 g, each), cut up	8	8
Peach Schnapps liqueur	2 tbsp.	30 mL

Combine cream and drink crystals in heavy medium saucepan. Stir until crystals are dissolved.

Add white chocolate. Heat and stir on medium-low until smooth. Do not overheat. Remove from heat.

Add Schnapps. Stir. Carefully pour into fondue pot. Place over low heat. Makes 1 cup (250 mL).

2 tbsp. (30 mL): 175 Calories; 9.3 g Total Fat; 33 mg Sodium; 2 g Protein; 22 g Carbohydrate; 0 g Dietary Fiber

Suggested dippers: Mini-Cakes, page 112; Macaroons, page 113; Popcorn Clusters, page 118; Tiny Ginger Cookies, page 119; angel food and chiffon cake chunks; chocolate cake chunks; strawberries; un-iced brownie cubes.

Chocolate Caramel Fondue

The buttery fudge taste of Halloween.

Skim evaporated milk	3/4 cup	175 mL
Caramel candies (about 1 lb., 454 g), unwrapped	58	58
Vanilla	1 tsp.	5 mL
Bittersweet chocolate baking squares (1 oz., 28 g, each), cut up	2	2

Heat evaporated milk in medium saucepan on medium-low until hot. Add caramels. Heat and stir until melted. Stir in vanilla.

(continued on next page)

Add chocolate. Stir until melted. Carefully pour into fondue pot. Place over very low heat as this burns easily. Makes 1 3/4 cups (425 mL) sauce.

2 tbsp. (30 mL): 151 Calories; 4.7 g Total Fat; 93 mg Sodium; 3 g Protein; 27 g Carbohydrate; 1 g Dietary Fiber

Suggested dippers: Ladyfingers, page 116; Crispy Rice Dippers, page 120; apple wedges; canned fruit, well-drained; cake chunks; marshmallows; un-iced brownie cubes.

Swiss Chocolate Fondue

A Toblerone chocolate bar lasts longer in the fondue pot than outside of it!

Swiss chocolate bar, broken up	12 oz.	340 g
Half-and-half (or whipping) cream	1/4 cup	60 mL
Kahlúa (or Crème de Menthe, Kirsch or Amaretto)	2 1/2 tbsp.	37 mL

Combine chocolate and cream in heavy medium saucepan. Heat and stir on medium-low until smooth.

Stir in Kahlúa. Carefully pour into fondue pot. Place over low heat. Makes 1 1/3 cups (325 mL).

2 tbsp. (30 mL): 176 Calories; 10 g Total Fat; 28 mg Sodium; 2 g Protein; 20 g Carbohydrate; 1 g Dietary Fiber

Suggested dippers: Chocolate Bites, page 118; banana chunks; pineapple chunks; strawberries; cake chunks; marshmallows.

Apricot Fondue

A pleasant apricot flavor with a delicate cinnamon aftertaste. No heat is necessary, as this can be served at room temperature, but is nice warmed as well.

Can of apricots, with juice	14 oz.	398 mL
Cornstarch	1 tbsp.	15 mL
Granulated sugar	1/4 cup	60 mL
Ground cinnamon	1/8 tsp.	0.5 mL
Skim evaporated milk	1/3 cup	75 mL

Process first 4 ingredients in blender until smooth. Pour into small saucepan. Heat and stir on medium until boiling and thickened.

Stir in evaporated milk. Heat through. Cool. Serve warm or at room temperature. Makes 2 cups (500 mL).

2 tbsp. (30 mL): 30 Calories; 0 g Total Fat; 7 mg Sodium; 1 g Protein; 7 g Carbohydrate; trace Dietary Fiber

Pictured on page 107.

Suggested dippers: Best French Toast, page 44; Tiny Puffs, page 115; Tiny Ginger Cookies, page 119; banana chunks; honeydew melon chunks; seedless grapes; cake chunks.

Strawberry Fondue

Creamy strawberry, a little bit tart.

Sliced fresh strawberries	2 cups	500 mL
Frozen concentrated orange juice	1 tbsp.	15 mL
Icing (confectioner's) sugar	2 tbsp.	30 mL
Prepared dessert topping	1 cup	250 mL

Purée strawberries, orange juice and icing sugar in blender. Strain, if desired, into fondue pot. Discard solids. Place over low heat.

Add dessert topping just before serving. Swirl with knife through strawberry mixture. Makes 1 2/3 cups (400 mL).

2 tbsp. (30 mL): 32 Calories; 1.5 g Total Fat; 2 mg Sodium; trace Protein; 5 g Carbohydrate; 1 g Dietary Fiber

(continued on next page)

Dessert Fondues

Pictured on page 107.

Suggested dippers: Mini-Cakes, page 112; Macaroons, page 113; Tiny Puffs, page 115; seedless grapes; chocolate cake chunks; marshmallows; un-iced brownie cubes.

Bumbleberry Fondue

A very good fondue with just a hint of sherry.

Can of raspberries, drained and 1/3 cup (75 mL) juice reserved	14 oz.	398 mL
Can of strawberries, drained and 1/3 cup (75 mL) juice reserved	14 oz.	398 mL
Can of blueberries, drained and 1/3 cup (75 mL) juice reserved	14 oz.	398 mL
Cornstarch	2 tbsp.	30 mL
Reserved fruit juices	1 cup	250 mL
Granulated sugar	1 tbsp.	15 mL
Sour cream	1/2 cup	125 mL
Sherry (or alcohol-free sherry)	1 tbsp.	15 mL

Process first 5 ingredients in blender until smooth. Strain if desired, into medium saucepan. Discard solids.

Add sugar. Heat and stir on medium until boiling and thickened.

Stir in sour cream and sherry. Carefully pour into fondue pot. Place over low heat. Makes 3 cups (750 mL).

2 tbsp. (30 mL): 50 Calories; 0.8 g Total Fat; 3 mg Sodium; trace Protein; 11 g Carbohydrate; 1 g Dietary Fiber

Suggested dippers: Biscuit Bites, page 88; Mini-Cakes, page 112; Wee Cookies, page 114; Tiny Puffs, page 115; banana chunks; honeydew melon chunks; pink and white marshmallows.

Cherry Fondue

Pleasantly sweet with a combination of cherry and almond that works well.

Can of cherry pie filling	19 oz.	540 mL
Apple juice	1/4 cup	60 mL
Milk	1/4 cup	60 mL
Almond flavoring	1/8 tsp.	0.5 mL
Granulated sugar	2 tbsp.	30 mL
Cornstarch	1 tbsp.	15 mL

Process all 6 ingredients in blender until smooth. Pour into medium saucepan. Heat and stir on medium-low until boiling and thickened. Carefully pour into fondue pot. Place over low heat or serve at room temperature. Makes 2 3/4 cups (675 mL).

2 tbsp. (30 mL): 38 Calories; 0.1 g Total Fat; 4 mg Sodium; trace Protein; 9 g Carbohydrate; trace Dietary Fiber

Pictured on page 125 and on back cover.

Suggested dippers: Chocolate Doughnut Holes, page 43; Tiny Puffs, page 115; Ladyfingers, page 116; peach slices; cake chunks; chocolate cookie pieces; un-iced brownie cubes.

1. Strawberry Fondue, page 104
2. (Fruit dippers)
3. Macaroons, page 113
4. Apricot Fondue, page 104
5. Tiny Puffs, page 115
6. Wee Cookies, page 114

Props Courtesy Of: Stokes
                     The Bay

Lemon Fondue

A light and creamy sweet fondue.

Water	1 1/4 cups	300 mL
Cornstarch	2 tbsp.	30 mL
Frozen concentrated lemon juice, thawed	1/2 cup	125 mL
Granulated sugar	2 tbsp.	30 mL
Hard margarine (or butter)	1/4 cup	60 mL
Prepared dessert topping	1 cup	250 mL

Stir water into cornstarch in medium saucepan until smooth. Add lemon juice, sugar and margarine. Heat and stir until boiling and thickened. Carefully pour into fondue pot.

Add dessert topping. Swirl through with knife until foamy. Place over low heat. Makes 2 1/3 cups (575 mL).

2 tbsp. (30 mL): 45 Calories; 3.6 g Total Fat; 31 mg Sodium; trace Protein; 3 g Carbohydrate; trace Dietary Fiber

Suggested dippers: Best French Toast, page 44; Tiny Puffs, page 115; Tiny Ginger Cookies, page 119; strawberries; cake chunks; fig-filled cookies; marshmallows.

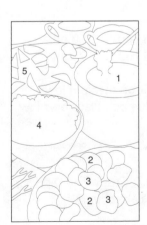

1. Caramel Fondue, page 110
2. Mini-Cakes, page 112
3. Chocolate Bites, page 118
4. Popcorn Clusters, page 118
5. (Fruit dippers)

Caramel Fondue

No candies to unwrap! Best used within 30 to 45 minutes of being made.

Can of sweetened condensed milk	11 oz.	300 mL
Corn syrup	1/4 cup	60 mL
Brown sugar, packed	1 cup	250 mL
Hard margarine (or butter)	1/2 cup	125 mL

Combine all 4 ingredients in medium saucepan. Heat and stir on medium-low until boiling. Boil for 5 minutes, stirring constantly to prevent scorching. If becomes too thick, add approximately 1/4 cup (60 mL) half-and-half cream or evaporated milk to thin to desired consistency. Carefully pour into fondue pot. Place over low heat. Makes 2 cups (500 mL).

2 tbsp. (30 mL): 195 Calories; 7.8 g Total Fat; 106 mg Sodium; 2 g Protein; 31 g Carbohydrate; 0 g Dietary Fiber

Pictured on page 108.

Suggested dippers: Tiny Puffs, page 115; Popcorn Clusters, page 118; Crispy Rice Dippers, page 120; banana chunks; fig-filled cookies; white cake chunks.

Peanut Butter Fondue

The perfect balance of peanut butter and chocolate.

Can of sweetened condensed milk	11 oz.	300 mL
Unsweetened chocolate baking squares	3	3
(1 oz., 28 g, each), chopped		
Milk	1/4 cup	60 mL
Smooth peanut butter	1/3 cup	75 mL

Combine all 4 ingredients in medium saucepan. Heat on medium-low, stirring often, until smooth. Carefully pour into fondue pot. Place over low heat. Makes 2 cups (500 mL).

2 tbsp. (30 mL): 135 Calories; 7.6 g Total Fat; 58 mg Sodium; 4 g Protein; 15 g Carbohydrate; 1 g Dietary Fiber

Suggested dippers: Peanut Butter Cookies, page 117; Crispy Rice Dippers, page 120; apple wedges; banana chunks; chocolate cake chunks; marshmallows.

Marmalade Fondue

At room temperature, this fondue does double duty
as a dipping sauce.

Three-fruit marmalade	1 cup	250 mL
Coarsely chopped red pepper	2 tbsp.	30 mL
Garlic clove (or 1/4 tsp., 1 mL, powder)	1	1
Lime juice	2 tsp.	10 mL
Chili paste	1/4 – 1/2 tsp.	1 – 2 mL

Process all 5 ingredients in blender until smooth. Pour into small saucepan. Heat and stir until hot. Carefully pour into fondue pot. Place over low heat. Makes 1 cup (250 mL).

2 tbsp. (30 mL): 102 Calories; 0 g Total Fat; 24 mg Sodium; trace Protein; 27 g Carbohydrate; trace Dietary Fiber

Pictured on page 18.

Suggested dippers: Reuben Gems, page 22; Biscuit Bites, page 88; toast triangles; white cake chunks.

 Keep apple wedges and bananas chunks from browning by soaking for five minutes in a 2/3 water and 1/3 lemon juice mixture.

Black Currant Fondue

Captures the taste of late summer.
Also makes a tasty dipping sauce at room temperature.

Black currant jelly	1/2 cup	125 mL
Marsala wine	3 tbsp.	50 mL
Grated lemon peel	1 tbsp.	15 mL
Lemon juice	1 tbsp.	15 mL
Candied ginger, minced	1 tbsp.	15 mL
Water	1/4 cup	60 mL
Cornstarch	2 tsp.	10 mL

Heat and stir jelly in saucepan on low until melted.

Add wine, lemon peel, lemon juice and candied ginger. Stir until combined.

Stir water into cornstarch in small cup until smooth. Gradually stir into jelly mixture. Heat and stir on medium until boiling and thickened. Carefully pour into fondue pot. Place over low heat. Makes 7/8 cup (200 mL).

1 tbsp. (15 mL): 36 Calories; 0 g Total Fat; 5 mg Sodium; trace Protein; 9 g Carbohydrate; trace Dietary Fiber

Pictured on page 36.

Suggested dippers: Biscuit Bites, page 88; Wee Cookies, page 114; toast triangles.

Mini-Cakes

These tiny pancakes go especially well with the fruit-based dessert fondues.

Large egg	1	1
Milk	1/4 cup	60 mL
Granulated sugar	1 tsp.	5 mL
Cooking oil	1 tsp.	5 mL
All-purpose flour	6 tbsp.	100 mL
Baking powder	3/4 tsp.	4 mL
Salt, just a pinch		

(continued on next page)

Beat egg, milk, sugar and cooking oil together in medium bowl.

Stir in flour until smooth. Add baking powder and salt. Mix. Drop by teaspoonfuls onto hot greased frying pan. Heat until bubbly on top and edges appear dry. Turn over to brown other side. Makes 26 mini-cakes.

1 mini-cake: 13 Calories; 0.4 g Total Fat; 14 mg Sodium; 1 g Protein; 2 g Carbohydrate; trace Dietary Fiber

Pictured on page 108.

Suggested fondues: Mocha Cherry Fondue, page 100; Peachy White Chocolate Fondue, page 102; Strawberry Fondue, page 104; Bumbleberry Fondue, page 105.

Macaroons

Almond flavor nicely complements a chocolate or fruit-based dessert fondue.

Egg whites (large), room temperature	2	2
Granulated sugar	1/3 cup	75 mL
Icing (confectioner's) sugar	1/3 cup	75 mL
Ground almonds	2 cups	500 mL
Vanilla	1/2 tsp.	2 mL

Beat egg whites in medium bowl until stiff peaks form.

Fold in both sugars, almonds and vanilla. Shape into 3/4 inch (2 cm) balls. Place on greased baking sheet. Bake in 325°F (160°C) oven for about 12 minutes until golden. Makes 60 macaroons.

1 macaroon: 21 Calories; 1.2 g Total Fat; 2 mg Sodium; 1 g Protein; 2 g Carbohydrate; 0 g Dietary Fiber

Pictured on page 107.

Suggested fondues: Raspberry Chocolate Fondue, page 99; Peachy White Chocolate Fondue, page 102; Strawberry Fondue, page 104.

Wee Cookies

Slightly crunchy on the outside and soft in the middle. Delectable.

Hard margarine (or butter), softened	1/4 cup	60 mL
Granulated sugar	1/2 cup	125 mL
Large egg	1	1
Milk	2 tbsp.	30 mL
Vanilla	1/2 tsp.	2 mL
All-purpose flour	1 1/2 cups	375 mL
Baking powder	1 1/2 tsp.	7 mL
Salt	1/4 tsp.	1 mL

Cream margarine, sugar and egg together in large bowl until smooth.

Add milk and vanilla. Mix.

Add flour, baking powder and salt. Mix well. Turn out onto lightly floured surface. Roll out to 1/4 inch (6 mm) thickness. Cut into shapes, using 1 to 1 1/2 inch (2.5 to 3.8 cm) cookie cutters. Arrange on ungreased baking sheet. Bake in 375°F (190°C) oven for 8 to 10 minutes until edges start to turn golden. Makes 48 cookies.

1 cookie: 35 Calories; 1.2 g Total Fat; 38 mg Sodium; 1 Protein; 5 g Carbohydrate; trace Dietary Fiber

Pictured on page 107.

Suggested fondues: Bumbleberry Fondue, page 105; Black Currant Fondue, page 112.

Paré Pointer
The famous writer disconnected his doorbell. He wanted to win the no-bell prize.

Tiny Puffs

These will remind you of French toast with their egg flavor and moist insides.

Water	1/2 cup	125 mL
Hard margarine (or butter)	1/4 cup	60 mL
Salt	1/8 tsp.	0.5 mL
All-purpose flour	1/2 cup	125 mL
Large eggs	2	2

Combine water, margarine and salt in medium saucepan. Bring to a boil.

Add flour. Stir vigorously until mixture pulls away from sides of pan. Remove from heat.

Add eggs, 1 at a time, beating well after each addition. Drop by level teaspoonfuls onto greased baking sheet, 1 inch (2.5 cm) apart. Bake in 400°F (205°C) oven for 8 to 10 minutes until edges appear golden. Remove to wire racks to cool. Makes about 75 puffs.

1 puff: 11 Calories; 0.8 g Total Fat; 13 mg Sodium; trace Protein; 1 g Carbohydrate; trace Dietary Fiber

Pictured on page 107.

SAVORY PUFFS: Add 3 tbsp. (50 mL) grated Parmesan cheese.

Suggested fondues: Parmesan Fondue, page 76; Emmenthaler Fondue, page 78; Tomato Soup Cheese Fondue, page 81; Mocha Cherry Fondue, page 100; Brandied Mocha Fondue, page 100; Apricot Fondue, page 104; Strawberry Fondue, page 104; Bumbleberry Fondue, page 105; Cherry Fondue, page 106; Lemon Fondue, page 109; Caramel Fondue, page 110.

Ladyfingers

Cookies with a sweet vanilla flavor that beg to be dipped into chocolate.

Egg white (large), room temperature	1	1
Granulated sugar	4 tsp.	20 mL
Egg yolk (large)	1	1
Granulated sugar	4 tsp.	20 mL
Vanilla	1/4 tsp.	1 mL
All-purpose flour	1/3 cup	75 mL

Beat egg white in small bowl until soft peaks form. Gradually add first amount of sugar, while beating, until stiff.

Beat egg yolk, second amount of sugar and vanilla in separate small bowl until light in color. Fold in egg white mixture.

Gradually fold in flour. Spoon into piping bag. Pipe into strips or other shapes onto greased baking sheet. Bake in 350°F (175°C) oven for about 12 minutes. Cool. Makes about 54 cookies.

1 cookie: 7 Calories; 0.1 g Total Fat; 1 mg Sodium; trace Protein; 1 g Carbohydrate; trace Dietary Fiber

Pictured on page 125.

Variation: Pipe into rosettes. Makes 40 rosettes.

Suggested fondues: Milky Chocolate Fondue, page 98; Brandied Mocha Fondue, page 100; Chocolate Caramel Fondue, page 102; Cherry Fondue, page 106.

Paré Pointer

The white cat won the milk drinking contest by six laps.

Peanut Butter Cookies

A soft cookie with nice peanut flavor that is not too sweet.
Pass the chocolate fondue, please.

Large egg	1	1
Hard margarine (or butter), softened	1/3 cup	75 mL
Brown sugar, packed	1/2 cup	125 mL
Smooth peanut butter	1/3 cup	75 mL
Finely chopped peanuts (optional)	1/3 cup	75 mL
All-purpose flour	1 cup	250 mL
Baking powder	1 tsp.	5 mL
Salt	1/8 tsp.	0.5 mL

Beat egg, margarine and brown sugar together in medium bowl until smooth.

Add peanut butter and peanuts. Mix well.

Add flour, baking powder and salt. Mix. Shape into 1 tsp. (5 mL) balls. Arrange on ungreased baking sheet. Press lightly with floured or wet fork. Bake in 350°F (175°C) oven for about 8 minutes. Makes 80 cookies.

1 cookie: 26 Calories; 1.5 g Total Fat; 25 mg Sodium; 1 g Protein; 3 g Carbohydrate; trace Dietary Fiber

Pictured on page 125 and on back cover.

Suggested fondues: Milky Chocolate Fondue, page 98; Chocolate Solo Fondue, page 101; Peanut Butter Fondue, page 110.

 Remember to store your fondue burner and fuel out of reach of children. The fondue burner should be empty for storage.

Chocolate Bites

Yummy, soft and moist cookies that will taste even better when dipped in any of the dessert fondues.

Hard margarine (or butter), softened	2 tbsp.	30 mL
Brown sugar, packed	1/4 cup	60 mL
Large egg, fork-beaten	1	1
Milk	1 tbsp.	15 mL
Cocoa	2 tbsp.	30 mL
Vanilla	1/4 tsp.	1 mL
Chopped walnuts (or pecans), optional	2 tbsp.	30 mL
All-purpose flour	1/2 cup	125 mL
Baking powder	1/4 tsp.	1 mL
Salt	1/8 tsp.	0.5 mL

Cream margarine, brown sugar, egg and milk together in medium bowl. Add cocoa. Beat until well mixed. Add vanilla and walnuts. Stir.

Add flour, baking powder and salt. Mix. Drop by 1/2 tsp. (2 mL) onto greased baking sheet. Bake in 350°F (175°C) oven for about 10 minutes. Makes about 72 cookies.

1 cookie: 11 Calories; 0.4 g Total Fat; 11 mg Sodium; trace Protein; 2 g Carbohydrate; trace Dietary Fiber

Pictured on page 108.

Suggested fondues: Raspberry Chocolate Fondue, page 99; Brandied Mocha Fondue, page 100; Swiss Chocolate Fondue, page 103.

Popcorn Clusters

Great candied popcorn in bite-size pieces for easy dipping.

Hard margarine (or butter)	2 tbsp.	30 mL
Large marshmallows, cut in half	16	16
Popped corn (3 tbsp., 50 mL, unpopped)	5 cups	1.25 L

(continued on next page)

Combine margarine and marshmallows in large saucepan. Heat and stir until melted and smooth. Remove from heat.

Add popped corn. Stir to coat completely. Form small clusters, using about 3 pieces of popped corn each, with greased hands. Cool on waxed paper. Makes about 72 clusters.

1 cluster: 20 Calories; 1 g Total Fat; 9 mg Sodium; trace Protein; 4 g Carbohydrate; trace Dietary Fiber

Pictured on page 108.

Suggested fondue: Raspberry Chocolate Fondue, page 99; Peachy White Chocolate Fondue, page 102; Caramel Fondue, page 110.

Tiny Ginger Cookies

Just what you hope for in a ginger cookie—flavorful and moist. So good you may not want to dip them.

Hard margarine (or butter), softened	1/4 cup	60 mL
Granulated sugar	1/4 cup	60 mL
Large egg, fork-beaten	1	1
Fancy (mild) molasses	1/4 cup	60 mL
Milk	3 tbsp.	50 mL
All-purpose flour	1 1/4 cups	300 mL
Baking soda	1/2 tsp.	2 mL
Ground ginger	1/4 tsp.	1 mL
Ground cinnamon	1/4 tsp.	1 mL
Salt	1/8 tsp.	0.5 mL

Cream first 5 ingredients together in medium bowl until smooth.

Combine remaining 5 ingredients in small bowl. Add to margarine mixture. Mix. Drop by teaspoonfuls onto greased baking sheet. Bake in 375°F (190°C) oven for 7 to 8 minutes until golden. Makes about 60 cookies.

1 cookie: 26 Calories; 0.9 g Total Fat; 27 mg Sodium; trace Protein; 4 g Carbohydrate; trace Dietary Fiber

Pictured on page 125 and on back cover.

Suggested fondues: Peachy White Chocolate Fondue, page 102; Apricot Fondue, page 104; Lemon Fondue, page 109.

Crispy Rice Dippers

Snap, crackle and pop—the kids won't be the only ones who like this dipper.

Hard margarine (or butter)	2 tbsp.	30 mL
Large marshmallows, cut in half	16	16
Corn syrup	2 tbsp.	30 mL
Chocolate drink powder	1/4 cup	60 mL
Crisp rice cereal (such as Rice Krispies)	3 1/2 cups	875 mL

Melt margarine in large saucepan. Add marshmallows, corn syrup and chocolate powder. Heat and stir until marshmallows are melted. Remove from heat.

Add rice cereal. Stir to coat cereal completely. Pack into greased 9 x 9 inch (22 x 22 cm) pan. Let stand for 3 to 4 hours. Cut into 1 x 1 inch (2.5 x 2.5 cm) squares. Makes 81 squares.

1 square: 18 Calories; 0.5 g Total Fat; 24 mg Sodium; trace Protein; 4 g Carbohydrate; trace Dietary Fiber

Pictured on page 125 and on back cover.

Suggested fondues: Chocolate Caramel Fondue, page 102; Caramel Fondue, page 110; Peanut Butter Fondue, page 110.

Paré Pointer

I'd love to tell you a joke about a pencil but it doesn't have any point.

Dessert Fondues

Tabletop Cooking

There are several exotic tabletop cooking options available such as the stone grill, chafing dish and flambé pan. Like a double boiler, a chafing dish often comes with a blazer pan and a warming pan. A flambé pan is usually more shallow than a chafing dish and looks more like a frying pan since it has a handle. In fact, a frying pan with a heat proof handle could be used if necessary. A flambé pan is just a variation of a chafing dish, so not everything made in it must be flaming! A stone grill looks like an extra wide ceramic tile, usually with two fuel burners beneath. The stone grill needs to be preheated in the oven prior to use, then placed on a rack over a heat source. Always read the manufacturer's instructions prior to use.

Omelet Supreme

The chafing dish is great for brunch when company's coming. Cooking over the boiling water means you can forget about it while you attend to other tasks. This omelet can serve 8 if there are other brunch items.

Sliced fresh mushrooms	2 cups	500 mL
Diced cooked ham, 1/2 inch (12 mm)	1 cup	250 mL
Hard margarine (or butter)	1 tbsp.	15 mL
Large eggs	10	10
Milk	1/2 cup	125 mL
Green onions, chopped	2	2
Salt	1 tsp.	5 mL
Pepper	1/4 tsp.	1 mL
Grated sharp Cheddar cheese	2/3 cup	150 mL

Put boiling water into water pan in chafing dish. Set over high flame. Set greased blazer pan inside water pan. Cover. Allow blazer pan to warm. Sauté mushrooms and ham in margarine in frying pan on medium-high for 3 to 4 minutes until browned and liquid from mushrooms has evaporated. Turn into blazer pan. Spread evenly. Cover.

Beat eggs, milk, green onion, salt and pepper together in medium bowl. Add to mushroom mixture. Cover. Cook over simmering water, without stirring, for 50 minutes until almost set.

Sprinkle cheese over egg mixture. Cover. Cook until egg is set and cheese is melted. Cuts into 6 wedges.

1 wedge: 251 Calories; 17.1 g Total Fat; 933 mg Sodium; 20 g Protein; 4 g Carbohydrate; trace Dietary Fiber

Coq Au Vin

A rich wine gravy forms while this well-known dish is cooking in the chafing dish. Takes a bit of time but makes a wonderful presentation for guests. Delicious served over mashed potatoes or noodles.

Tiny white pearl onions	20 oz.	560 g
Boiling water	3 cups	750 mL
Ice water		
All-purpose flour	1/4 cup	60 mL
Seasoned salt	1/2 tsp.	2 mL
Freshly ground pepper	1/4 tsp.	1 mL
Paprika	1 tsp.	5 mL
Boneless, skinless chicken breast halves, sliced diagonally	2 lbs.	900 g
Bacon slices, cut into 1 inch (2.5 cm) pieces	5	5
Whole fresh small mushrooms (or medium, cut in half)	3 cups	750 mL
Garlic cloves, minced (or 1/2 tsp., 2 mL, powder)	2	2
Dry red (or alcohol-free) wine	1 cup	250 mL
Bay leaf	1	1
Ground thyme	1/4 tsp.	1 mL
Fresh parsley, for garnish		

Add onions to boiling water in medium saucepan. Boil for 5 minutes. Drain. Immediately cool in ice water. Cut thin slice from root end. Squeeze from stem end to pop out onion. Set aside. Makes about 2 cups (500 mL) peeled onions.

Combine next 4 ingredients in shallow dish. Add chicken pieces. Stir until well coated.

(continued on next page)

Fry bacon in covered blazer pan or chafing dish, stirring several times, until browned. Remove bacon to paper towel to drain. Set aside. Spoon off and reserve all but 2 tbsp. (30 mL) bacon drippings. Brown coated chicken in bacon drippings over high flame, turning several times. Add up to 2 tsp. (10 mL) reserved drippings if needed. Sprinkle any remaining seasoned flour over chicken. Cover. Cook for 5 minutes. Stir.

Add onions, mushrooms and garlic. Cover. Cook over high flame for 5 minutes. Stir.

Add wine, bay leaf and thyme. Stir. Cover. Cook over high flame for about 45 minutes, stirring once or twice, until chicken is no longer pink and gravy is thickened. Remove and discard bay leaf. Add bacon. Stir gently.

Sprinkle with parsley just before serving. Serves 6.

1 serving: 336 Calories; 9.9 g Total Fat; 190 mg Sodium; 38 g Protein; 16 g Carbohydrate; 2 g Dietary Fiber

Although we use chicken in Coq Au Vin, above, the recipe was traditionally made with a rooster that was at least twelve months old. The red wine was necessary to tenderize the meat, however now we use wine for the flavor it adds. When preparing raw chicken (or rooster) remember to always wash your hands, countertops, cutting boards, knives and other utensils with soapy water before and after they come in contact with other foods.

Hot Crab Cheese Dip

Prepare in the flambé pan and serve with an assortment of crackers.

Cream cheese	8 oz.	250 g
Light salad dressing (or mayonnaise)	1/4 cup	60 mL
Garlic clove, crushed (or 1/4 tsp., 1 mL, powder)	1	1
Green onions, finely chopped	2	2
Hot pepper sauce, dash		
Cans of crabmeat (4 1/4 oz., 120 g, each), drained, cartilage removed, flaked	2	2
Freshly ground pepper, sprinkle		

Slowly melt cream cheese in flambé pan over high flame, stirring constantly.

Add salad dressing, garlic, green onion and hot pepper sauce. Stir.

Add crab and pepper. Stir. Heat until hot but not boiling. Keep warm over low flame. Makes 2 1/4 cups (550 mL).

1 tbsp. (15 mL): 33 Calories; 2.9 g Total Fat; 72 mg Sodium; 1 g Protein; trace Carbohydrate; trace Dietary Fiber

1. (Fruit dippers)
2. Milky Chocolate Fondue, page 98
3. Tiny Ginger Cookies, page 119
4. Peanut Butter Cookies, page 117
5. Ladyfingers, page 116
6. Crispy Rice Dippers, page 120
7. Cherry Fondue, page 106

Props Courtesy Of: Stokes
The Bay

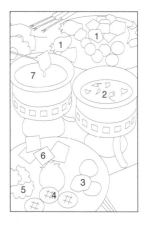

Tabletop Cooking

Hot Chili Cheese Dip

Serve this delicious dip in the chafing dish with plenty of tortilla chips.
Recipe should be doubled for a large crowd. It goes fast!

Can of chili with beans	14 oz.	398 mL
Can of diced tomatoes, with juice	14 oz.	398 mL
Pasteurized cheese loaf (such as	1 lb.	454 g
Velveeta), cubed (about 4 cups, 1 L)		
Can of diced green chilies, with liquid	4 oz.	114 mL
Garlic cloves, minced (or 1/2 tsp.,	2	2
2 mL, powder)		
Hot pepper sauce, dash		

Combine chili with beans and tomatoes with juice in blazer pan of chafing dish. Mash to break up beans and tomatoes.

Add remaining 4 ingredients. Heat and stir over high flame for about 15 minutes until cheese is melted. Place over hot water in water pan over medium flame to keep hot. Makes 5 1/2 cups (1.4 L).

1 tbsp. (15 mL): 24 Calories; 1.6 g Total Fat; 127 mg Sodium; 1 g Protein; 1 g Carbohydrate; trace Dietary Fiber

Crêpes Suzette, page 133

Props Courtesy Of: A Taste Of Provence

Asparagus And Crab Soup

Prepared in the chafing dish, this has an Oriental look with the egg threads in the broth.

Fresh asparagus	1 lb.	454 g
Large garlic clove, minced (or 1/4 tsp., 1 mL, powder)	1	1
Green onions, sliced	2	2
Cooking oil	2 tbsp.	30 mL
Can of crabmeat, drained, cartilage removed	6 oz.	170 g
Cans of condensed chicken broth (10 oz., 284 mL, each)	2	2
Water	1 1/4 cups	300 mL
Cornstarch	3 tbsp.	50 mL
Large egg	1	1
Salt	1/2 tsp.	2 mL
Pepper, sprinkle		
Green onions, sliced (for garnish)	2	2

Wash and trim asparagus, discarding woody ends. Steam for about 3 minutes over boiling water until bright green and tender-crisp. Chill quickly under cold water. Cut into diagonal 1 inch (2.5 cm) pieces. Set aside.

Sauté garlic and first amount of green onion in cooking oil in blazer pan of chafing dish over high flame until hot.

Add crab. Heat and stir for 3 minutes.

Stir in chicken broth. Cover. Cook over high flame for about 20 minutes until simmering.

Stir water into cornstarch in small bowl until smooth. Add to chicken broth mixture. Heat and stir until boiling and thickened.

Beat egg, salt and pepper together in small cup. Gradually stir egg mixture into soup. Stir for 1 minute. Add asparagus. Cover. Heat through, stirring occasionally.

(continued on next page)

Tabletop Cooking

Garnish with second amount of green onion. Makes 5 1/2 cups (1.4 L).

1 cup (250 mL): 141 Calories; 7.4 g Total Fat; 1030 mg Sodium; 10 g Protein; 9 g Carbohydrate; 1 g Dietary Fiber

---

Onion Soup

Richly flavored broth prepared in the chafing dish with just the right amount of onion. The cheese toast looks elegant atop the soup and can be made up to one hour ahead. Recipe can be doubled easily.

Cans of condensed beef broth (10 oz., 284 mL, each)	2	2
Hot water	1 1/2 cups	375 mL
Dry red (or alcohol-free) wine	1/2 cup	125 mL
Medium onions, thinly sliced (about 4 cups, 1 L)	3	3
Hard margarine (or butter)	1/4 cup	60 mL
Freshly ground pepper, heavy sprinkle		
Baguette bread slices, 1 inch (2.5 cm) thick	12	12
Grated part-skim mozzarella cheese	1 cup	250 mL
Grated Parmesan cheese	2 tbsp.	30 mL

Measure broth, hot water and wine into blazer pan of chafing dish. Cover. Heat over high flame.

Sauté onion in margarine in large frying pan on medium for about 15 minutes until onion is soft and golden. Add pepper. Stir. Add to broth mixture. Cover. Simmer over low flame for 1 hour. Makes 5 1/4 cups (1.3 L) soup.

Arrange baguette slices in single layer on ungreased baking sheet. Toast 1 side in oven under broiler until browned. Turn. Cover slices with mozzarella and Parmesan cheese. Broil until cheese is melted. Makes 12 cheese toast toppers. Place 2 pieces of cheese toast on top of individual servings of soup. Serves 6.

1 serving: 325 Calories; 14.2 g Total Fat; 1173 mg Sodium; 14 g Protein; 32 g Carbohydrate; 2 g Dietary Fiber

Cherries Jubilee

So good, so easy and so showy for company.
A spectacular dessert in the chafing dish.

Vanilla ice cream	4 cups	1 L
Reserved cherry juice	1 1/2 cups	375 mL
Granulated sugar	1/2 cup	125 mL
Cornstarch	3 tbsp.	50 mL
Salt, sprinkle		
Cans of pitted Bing (or dark) cherries (14 oz., 398 mL, each), juice reserved	3	3
Lemon juice	1 tbsp.	15 mL
Brandy (or Kirsch)	1/4 cup	60 mL
Sliced almonds, toasted, for garnish		

Scoop ice cream into small 2 to 2 1/2 inch (5 to 6.4 cm) balls. Place on large chilled baking sheet. Cover. Freeze. Makes about 16 ice cream balls.

Measure reserved cherry juice into blazer pan of chafing dish. Cover. Heat over high flame for about 10 minutes until simmering.

Combine sugar, cornstarch and salt in small bowl. Stir into simmering cherry juice until boiling and thickened. Cover.

Stir in cherries and lemon juice. Cover. Heat for 10 to 15 minutes, stirring occasionally, until cherries are heated through.

When ready to serve, pour brandy into center of cherries. Ignite with long match. Blue flames will burn about 20 seconds. Stir. Makes 4 1/2 cups (1.1 L). Arrange ice cream balls in individual chilled glass bowls. Spoon cherries and sauce over ice cream.

Sprinkle with almonds. Serves 8.

1 serving: 340 Calories; 7.8 g Total Fat; 67 mg Sodium; 4 g Protein; 63 g Carbohydrate; 2 g Dietary Fiber

Hot Cajun Shrimp

Serve this starter appetizer in a flambé pan with a basket of crusty rolls to help soak up all the spicy juices.

Butter (not margarine)	3 tbsp.	50 mL
Garlic cloves, minced (or 3/4 tsp., 4 mL, powder)	3	3
Medium shrimp (about 2 lbs., 900 g), peeled, deveined and blotted dry	3 1/2 cups	875 mL
Cajun seasoning	1 tbsp.	15 mL
Dried rosemary, crushed	1 tsp.	5 mL
Worcestershire sauce	1 tsp.	5 mL
Freshly squeezed lemon juice	3 tbsp.	50 mL
Fresh parsley, for garnish		
Finely grated lemon peel, for garnish	1 tsp.	5 mL

Melt butter in flambé pan over medium flame. Add garlic, shrimp and cajun seasoning. Cook until shrimp just starts to turn pink.

Add rosemary and Worcestershire sauce. Heat for about 8 minutes, stirring often, until shrimp are pink and curled.

Pour lemon juice over shrimp mixture. Stir. Sprinkle with parsley and lemon peel. Keep warm over low flame to serve. Serves 12.

1 serving: 110 Calories; 4.3 g Total Fat; 250 mg Sodium; 16 g Protein; 2 g Carbohydrate; Trace Dietary Fiber

Pictured on page 143.

Paré Pointer

The little pig felt like running away. He thought the rest of the pigs took him for grunted.

Ham And Mushroom Mounds

Make the filling in the flambé pan while the patty shells are baking.
Your dinner guests will be impressed with the elegant look and taste
of this easy-to-prepare dish.

Frozen patty shells	12	12
Hard margarine (or butter)	2 tsp.	10 mL
Sliced fresh mushrooms	1 1/2 cups	375 mL
Diced cooked ham (about 14 oz., 395 g)	2 cups	500 mL
Can of condensed cream of mushroom soup	10 oz.	284 mL
Dry white (or alcohol-free) wine	1/4 cup	60 mL
Can of sliced ripe olives, well drained	4.5 oz.	125 mL
Jar of sliced pimiento, drained and diced	2 oz.	57 mL
Light sour cream	1/2 cup	125 mL
Grated medium Cheddar cheese	1/2 cup	125 mL
Chopped fresh parsley, for garnish		

Cook patty shells according to package directions.

Melt margarine in flambé pan over high flame. Add mushrooms and ham. Heat and stir until liquid has evaporated.

Add soup, wine, olives and pimiento. Heat through until bubbling. Reduce flame.

Add sour cream and cheese. Stir for 2 minutes until cheese is melted. Do not boil. Makes 4 cups (1 L). Spoon 1/3 cup (75 mL) into each patty shell.

Garnish with parsley. Makes 12 mounds.

1 mound: 371 Calories; 25.3 g Total Fat; 712 mg Sodium; 10 g Protein; 25 g Carbohydrate; trace Dietary Fiber

Crêpes Suzette

Prepare this traditional flaming dessert in front of your guests in the flambé pan. Make the crêpes ahead of time. The butter sauce and reheating of the crêpes takes only about 15 minutes.

CRÊPES

All-purpose flour	2/3 cup	150 mL
Granulated sugar	2 tbsp.	30 mL
Salt, sprinkle		
Milk	1 cup	250 mL
Large eggs	4	4
Hard margarine (or butter), melted	2 tbsp.	30 mL

ORANGE BUTTER SAUCE

Butter (not margarine)	1/2 cup	125 mL
Granulated sugar	1/2 cup	125 mL
Grated orange peel	2 tsp.	10 mL
Freshly squeezed orange juice	1/3 cup	75 mL
Cointreau (or Triple Sec)	1/3 cup	75 mL

Crêpes: Combine all 6 ingredients in medium bowl. Beat until smooth. Spray small non-stick frying pan with cooking spray. Heat on medium. Measure 2 tbsp. (30 mL) batter into hot frying pan. Immediately swirl pan to spread batter evenly in bottom. Cook for 30 seconds until set and edges are brown. Turn over. Cook 20 to 30 seconds to brown second side. Layer cooked crêpes between sheets of waxed paper. When all have been made, fold each crêpe into quarters and arrange on plate. Cover until ready to use. Makes 18 crêpes.

Orange Butter Sauce: Place first 4 ingredients in blazer pan of chafing dish. Heat and stir over high flame until sugar is dissolved and sauce is bubbling. Place crêpes, slightly overlapping one another, in sauce. Heat crêpes, spooning sauce over and stirring gently around the crêpes, until they are warmed through. Drizzle Cointreau over top of crêpes. Ignite. Flame will disappear very quickly. Makes 1 1/4 cups (300 mL) sauce. Place 3 crêpes on individual dessert plates and spoon 3 tbsp. (50 mL) sauce over top. Serves 6.

1 serving: 421 Calories; 24 g Total Fat; 275 mg Sodium; 7 g Protein; 37 g Carbohydrate; 1 g Dietary Fiber

Pictured on page 126.

Shrimp And Scallop Newburg

Prepare in the flambé pan and serve with toast cups or patty shells.
Can easily be doubled to serve a crowd.

Dry white (or alcohol-free) wine (or apple juice)	1/2 cup	125 mL
Water	1/2 cup	125 mL
Bay leaf	1	1
Medium uncooked shrimp, peeled and deveined (about 50)	3/4 lb.	340 g
Medium uncooked scallops (about 50)	3/4 lb.	340 g
Butter (not margarine)	1/3 cup	75 mL
All-purpose flour	1/4 cup	60 mL
Whole milk (or half-and-half cream)	1 1/2 cups	375 mL
Egg yolks (large), fork-beaten	3	3
Sherry (or alcohol-free sherry)	1/3 cup	75 mL
Lemon juice	1 1/2 tsp.	7 mL
Salt	1/4 tsp.	1 mL
Paprika, sprinkle (optional)		
Freshly ground pepper, sprinkle		

Heat wine, water and bay leaf in medium saucepan until boiling.

Add shrimp and scallops. Cover. Return to a boil. Cook for 2 minutes. Stir. Cover. Cook for 2 minutes until shrimp are pink and curled, and scallops are opaque. Do not overcook. Remove seafood with slotted spoon to medium bowl. Strain liquid, reserving 3/4 cup (175 mL). Remove and discard bay leaf.

Melt butter in flambé pan over high flame until bubbling but not brown. Add flour. Stir until well mixed. Stir in reserved cooking liquid and milk. Heat and stir over high flame for about 12 minutes until thickened and hot.

(continued on next page)

Tabletop Cooking

Add 2 large spoonfuls of sauce to egg yolks. Stir well. Stir egg mixture back into sauce.

Add sherry, lemon juice and salt. Heat and stir until slightly thickened. Do not boil. Stir in shrimp and scallops.

Sprinkle with paprika and pepper. Keep warm over low flame. Makes 4 1/2 cups (1.1 L).

1 cup (250 mL): 425 Calories; 22.6 g Total Fat; 561 mg Sodium; 34 g Protein; 13 g Carbohydrate; trace Dietary Fiber

 To make a dish truly spectacular, flambéing does the trick every time. Use light or dark rum, fruit liqueur such as apricot, cherry or orange, or brandy with a high alcohol content. The food must be hot and the alcohol must be warm. If the liquor or liqueur is heated too long or is too hot, the alcohol will evaporate and won't ignite. Pour the alcohol over the food and use a long match for igniting. The flames will go out when all the alcohol is burned away, leaving just the taste.

Paré Pointer
The teacher said the clock had to go. It tocked too much.

Pork And Apple Kabobs

This pork has a definite garlic flavor. Prepare on the hot stone grill and serve with Orange Sauce, page 60.

Dry mustard	1 tsp.	5 mL
Prepared orange juice	1 cup	250 mL
Garlic cloves, minced (or 1/2 tsp., 2 mL, powder)	2	2
Pork tenderloin, cut into 3/4 inch (2 cm) cubes	3/4 lb.	340 g
Unpeeled cooking apples, (such as MacIntosh), cut into 1/2 x 1 1/2 inch (1.2 cm x 3.8 cm) slices (see Tip, page 111)	2	2
Medium red pepper, cubed same size as pork	1	1
Metal skewers, 8 inch (20 cm) length	10	10
Cooking oil	1 tsp.	5 mL

Combine mustard, orange juice and garlic in shallow dish or resealable plastic bag. Makes 1 cup (250 mL) marinade. Add pork. Stir to coat. Cover or seal. Marinate in refrigerator for at least 1 hour, turning several times.

Remove pork. Discard marinade. Alternate pork, apple and red pepper on skewers. Makes 10 kabobs.

Heat stone grill in oven according to manufacturer's instructions. Brush hot stone with cooking oil. Grill kabobs on stone over high flame for 12 minutes, turning often to cook all sides, until desired doneness.

1 kabob: 71 Calories; 1.5 g Total Fat; 17 mg Sodium; 8 g Protein; 6 g Carbohydrate; 1 g Dietary Fiber

Paré Pointer

If you are going to the desert, be sure to take a thirst-aid kit.

Caesar Seafood Kabobs

"Pretty-in-pink" shrimp and scallops cooked on the hot stone grill.

Clam tomato beverage	1 cup	250 mL
Celery salt	1/2 tsp.	2 mL
Salt	1/2 tsp.	2 mL
Lemon juice	1 tsp.	5 mL
Hot pepper sauce (such as Tobasco)	1/4 tsp.	1 mL
Pepper	1/4 tsp.	1 mL
Large uncooked shrimp, peeled and deveined (about 50)	1 lb.	454 g
Medium uncooked scallops (about 35)	1/2 lb.	225 g
Metal skewers, 4 inch (10 cm) length	16	16
Cooking oil	1 tsp.	5 mL

Combine clam tomato beverage, celery salt, salt, lemon juice, hot pepper sauce and pepper in large bowl. Makes 1 cup (250 mL) marinade.

Add shrimp and scallops to bowl. Stir to coat. Cover. Marinate in refrigerator for 30 minutes.

Remove shrimp and scallops. Discard marinade. Alternate shrimp and scallops on 16 metal skewers.

Heat stone grill in oven according to manufacturer's instructions. Brush hot stone with cooking oil. Grill kabobs on stone over high flame for 2 minutes per side. Makes 16 kabobs. Serves 8.

1 serving: 94 Calories; 1.8 g Total Fat; 218 mg Sodium; 16 g Protein; 2 g Carbohydrate; trace Dietary Fiber

Paré Pointer
No wonder it takes so long to get to the moon.
It's uphill all the way.

Lamb-On-A-Stick

This is a flavorful way to serve lamb on a hot stone grill. There's wonderful blend of spices to this marinade, and the mango provides a burst of sweet fruit.

Lime juice	2 tbsp.	30 mL
Olive (or cooking) oil	1 tbsp.	15 mL
Chopped red onion	1/4 cup	60 mL
Curry powder	1/4 tsp.	1 mL
Finely grated gingerroot	1 tsp.	5 mL
Ground cumin	1 tsp.	5 mL
Salt	1/2 tsp.	2 mL
Freshly ground pepper	1/4 tsp.	1 mL
Lamb shoulder, cubed	3/4 lb.	340 g
Medium green pepper, cubed same size as lamb	1	1
Mango (slightly underripe), cubed same size as lamb	1	1
Metal skewers, 4 inch (10 cm) length	8	8
Cooking oil	1 tsp.	5 mL

Combine first 8 ingredients in shallow dish or resealable plastic bag. Makes 2/3 cup (150 mL) marinade.

Add lamb to marinade. Turn to coat. Cover or seal. Marinate in refrigerator overnight.

Remove lamb. Discard marinade. Alternate lamb, green pepper and mango on skewers.

Heat stone grill in oven according to manufacturer's instructions. Brush hot stone with cooking oil. Grill kabobs on stone over high flame for about 15 minutes, turning often to cook all sides, until desired doneness. Makes 8 kabobs.

1 kabob: 89 Calories; 3.4 g Total Fat; 67 mg Sodium; 9 g Protein; 6 g Carbohydrate; 1 g Dietary Fiber

Tabletop Cooking

Sukiyaki Beef

Prepared on the hot stone grill, these tender strips of marinated beef have an Indonesian soy flavor with an underlying sweetness.

Cooking oil	2 tbsp.	30 mL
Brown sugar, packed	2 tbsp.	30 mL
Beef broth	1/2 cup	125 mL
Indonesian sweet soy sauce	1/3 cup	75 mL
Beef flank steak, cut into thin strips	1 lb.	454 g
Cooking oil	1 tsp.	5 mL
Bamboo skewers, 10 inch (25 cm) length, soaked in water for 10 minutes	4	4

Combine first amount of cooking oil, brown sugar, broth and soy sauce in small cup. Pour into shallow dish or resealable plastic bag. Makes about 1 cup (250 mL) marinade. Add beef. Turn to coat. Cover or seal. Marinate in refrigerator for 3 to 4 hours, turning once or twice.

Heat stone grill in oven according to manufacturer's instructions. Remove beef. Discard marinade. Brush hot stone with second amount of cooking oil. Thread beef strips on skewers. Grill on stone over high flame for 6 to 8 minutes, turning often to cook all sides. Serves 4.

1 serving: 231 Calories; 12.8 g Total Fat; 457 mg Sodium; 25 g Protein; 2 g Carbohydrate; 0 g Dietary Fiber

Pictured on page 144.

Paré Pointer

No wonder the skeleton climbed the tree. A dog was after its bones.

Stone Grill Chicken

Serve this as a main course or as an appetizer on the hot stone grill. Chicken is moist and tender. Flavor is pleasant.

Sesame seeds	1 tbsp.	15 mL
Garlic cloves, minced (or 1/2 tsp., 2 mL, powder)	2	2
Lemon juice	1 tsp.	5 mL
Chopped onion	1/2 cup	125 mL
Hard margarine (or butter), melted	2 tbsp.	30 mL
Soy sauce	1/4 cup	60 mL
Chili paste	1/4 tsp.	1 mL
Rice wine (sake)	1 tbsp.	15 mL
Granulated sugar	1 tbsp.	15 mL
Chicken broth	1/2 cup	125 mL
Boneless, skinless chicken breast halves (about 6), cubed	1 1/2 lbs.	680 g
Cooking oil	1 tsp.	5 mL

Combine first 10 ingredients in small bowl. Stir until sugar is dissolved. Makes 1 1/4 cups (300 mL) marinade. Pour into shallow dish or resealable plastic bag.

Add chicken. Stir to coat. Cover or seal. Marinate in refrigerator for several hours, turning once or twice.

Heat stone grill in oven according to manufacturer's instructions. Brush hot stone with cooking oil. Remove chicken. Discard marinade. Grill chicken on stone over high flame for about 6 minutes, turning often, until no pink remains. Serves 6.

1 serving: 151 Calories; 3.9 g Total Fat; 203 mg Sodium; 26 g Protein; 1 g Carbohydrate; trace Dietary Fiber

Pictured on page 144.

Go-Withs

Round out an oil or broth fondue with rice and salad. Supplement a chafing dish or hot stone grill appetizer with bread sticks and a beverage. These recipes are light enough on the palate to accentuate all kinds of tabletop cooking, and colorful enough to be pretty visual accents.

Fried Rice

Brown-colored rice with bits of green and red. Serve as a "go-with" for seafood or chicken fondue.

Chopped green onion	1/4 cup	60 mL
Chopped fresh mushrooms	1/2 cup	125 mL
Chopped red pepper	1/4 cup	60 mL
Cooking oil	2 tbsp.	30 mL
Frozen peas, thawed	1/2 cup	125 mL
Cooked and chilled long grain white rice (boil 1 1/2 cups, 375 mL, uncooked)	3 cups	750 mL
Soy sauce	3 tbsp.	50 mL

Sauté green onion, mushrooms and red pepper in cooking oil in frying pan for about 2 minutes.

Add peas, rice and soy sauce. Stir until heated through. Makes 3 1/4 cups (800 mL).

1/2 cup (125 mL): 186 Calories; 4.6 g Total Fat; 497 mg Sodium; 4 g Protein; 31 g Carbohydrate; 1 g Dietary Fiber

Pictured on page 143.

Marinated Tomato And Onion

Bright white and red contrasts. Great fresh flavor!

Tiny white pearl onions	20 oz.	560 g
Boiling water		
Fresh mint sprigs, finely chopped (about 1 tbsp., 15 mL)	3	3
Garlic clove, minced (or 1/4 tsp., 1 mL, powder)	1	1
White wine vinegar	3 tbsp.	50 mL
Olive (or cooking) oil	3 tbsp.	50 mL
Chopped fresh parsley (or 1 1/2 tsp., 7 mL, flakes)	2 tbsp.	30 mL
Salt	1/2 tsp.	2 mL
Freshly ground pepper, sprinkle		
Cherry tomatoes, halved	2 cups	500 mL

Add onions to boiling water in medium saucepan. Boil for 5 minutes. Drain. Immediately cool in ice water. Cut thin slice from root end. Squeeze from stem end to pop out onion. Set aside. Makes about 2 cups (500 mL) skinned onions.

Combine mint, garlic, wine vinegar, olive oil, parsley, salt and pepper in medium bowl. Add onions and tomatoes. Stir to coat well. Chill for at least 3 hours. Makes 3 1/2 cups (875 mL).

1/2 cup (125 mL): 83 Calories; 6.1 g Total Fat; 175 mg Sodium; 1 g Protein; 6 g Carbohydrate; 1 g Dietary Fiber

Pictured on page 144.

1. Spring Leaf Salad, page 146
2. Hot Cajun Shrimp, page 131
3. Fried Rice, page 141
4. Mulled Wine, page 149

Props Courtesy Of: Cherison Enterprises Inc.
                      Stokes

Go-Withs

Black Bean Rice Salad

Mild but tasty dressing. Salad has lots of color.

Cooked and cooled long grain white rice	3 cups	750 mL
Can of black beans, rinsed and drained	19 oz.	540 mL
Frozen corn, thawed and cooked	1 cup	250 mL
OIL AND VINEGAR DRESSING		
Olive (or cooking) oil	1/4 cup	60 mL
Red wine vinegar	2 tbsp.	30 mL
Chopped fresh parsley (or 2 tsp., 10 mL, flakes)	3 tbsp.	50 mL
Diced red onion	1/4 cup	60 mL
Garlic clove, minced (or 1/4 tsp., 1 mL, powder)	1	1
Salt	1/8 tsp.	0.5 mL
Pepper	1/8 tsp.	0.5 mL

Combine rice, beans and corn in large bowl.

Oil and Vinegar Dressing: Combine olive oil, wine vinegar, parsley, red onion, garlic, salt and pepper in small bowl. Makes 1/2 cup (125 mL) dressing. Add dressing to rice mixture. Stir until well coated. Chill for about 1 hour. Makes 6 1/2 cups (1.6 L).

1 cup (250 mL): 288 Calories; 9.5 g Total Fat; 148 mg Sodium; 7 g Protein; 44 g Carbohydrate; 3 g Dietary Fiber

Pictured on page 144.

1. Black Bean Rice Salad, above
2. Stone Grill Chicken, page 140
3. Plum Sauce, page 68
4. Sukiyaki Beef, page 139
5. Marinated Tomato And Onion, page 142
6. (Shrimp with) Fresh Herb And Wine Marinade, page 50

Spring Leaf Salad

Very pretty with lots of color and texture. Dressing is tangy and sweet all in one bite. Walnut oil is a special ingredient, worth the added expense.

Bag of mixed spring greens (about 12 cups, 3 L)	9 1/2 oz.	270 g
Peeled and cubed avocado (about 1 medium)	1 cup	250 mL
Lemon juice	2 tsp.	10 mL
Slivered red pepper (about 1 medium)	2 cups	500 mL
Sliced English cucumber, with peel (about 1/2)	1 1/3 cups	325 mL
Chopped green onion	1/4 cup	60 mL
Chopped fresh parsley (or 2 tsp., 10 mL, flakes)	3 tbsp.	50 mL
Diced Swiss cheese	1/2 cup	125 mL
Halved cherry tomatoes (about 12)	3/4 cup	175 mL
WALNUT DRESSING		
Walnut oil	3 tbsp.	50 mL
Cooking oil	3 tbsp.	50 mL
White wine vinegar	3 tbsp.	50 mL
Dry mustard	1/4 tsp.	1 mL
Granulated sugar	2 tsp.	10 mL
Salt, sprinkle		
Freshly ground pepper, sprinkle		

Wash and dry greens well. Put into large salad bowl.

Combine avocado and lemon juice in small bowl. Coat avocado well to prevent browning. Drain. Add avocado to greens.

Add next 6 ingredients. Stir.

Walnut Dressing: Combine both oils, wine vinegar, mustard, sugar, salt and pepper in small bowl. Pour over salad. Lightly toss to coat well. Serve immediately. Makes 15 cups (3.75 L).

1 cup (250 mL): 105 Calories; 9 g Total Fat; 21 mg Sodium; 2 g Protein; 5 g Carbohydrate; 1 g Dietary Fiber

Pictured on page 143.

Pineapple Mango Coleslaw

Lots of color to this fruity coleslaw. Not as tangy as traditional coleslaw but still good.

Butter lettuce leaves	5	5
Shredded red cabbage (about 1/2 head)	6 cups	1.5 L
Thinly sliced celery	1 cup	250 mL
Grated carrot	3/4 cup	175 mL
Can of pineapple chunks, drained and juice reserved	14 oz.	398 mL
Mango, peeled and chopped into chunks (about 1 cup, 250 mL)	1	1
PINEAPPLE DRESSING		
Light mayonnaise (or salad dressing)	1/4 cup	60 mL
Reserved pineapple juice	2 tbsp.	30 mL
Freshly squeezed lime juice	1 tbsp.	15 mL
Pistachios, shelled and chopped	1/3 cup	75 mL

Line salad bowl with lettuce leaves. Set aside.

Combine next 5 ingredients in large bowl. Set aside.

Pineapple Dressing: Combine first 3 ingredients in small bowl. Makes 7 tbsp. (115 mL) dressing. Add to cabbage mixture. Toss until well coated. Spoon cabbage mixture into lettuce leaves.

Sprinkle salad with pistachios just before serving. Makes 10 cups (2.5 L).

1 cup (250 mL): 104 Calories; 4.6 g Total Fat; 97 mg Sodium; 2 g Protein; 16 g Carbohydrate; 2 g Dietary Fiber

Pictured on page 71.

Pesto Feta Baguette

Basil and feta cheese combine for a great flavor in this soft-textured attractive loaf. Serve with cheese or tomato based fondues.

All-purpose flour	3 cups	750 mL
Instant yeast	2 1/2 tsp.	12 mL
Granulated sugar	1 tbsp.	15 mL
Salt	1 tsp.	5 mL
Very warm (not hot) milk	1 cup	250 mL
Very warm (not hot) water	1/2 cup	125 mL
Basil pesto	2 tbsp.	30 mL
All-purpose flour, approximately	1 cup	250 mL
Feta cheese, finely crumbled	1/2 cup	125 mL

Combine first amount of flour, yeast, sugar and salt in large bowl. Mix well.

Add milk, water and pesto. Beat for 2 minutes.

Add enough of second amount of flour until dough pulls away from sides of bowl.

Turn out dough onto lightly floured surface. Add cheese. Knead in cheese until dough is smooth and elastic. Place in greased bowl, turning once to grease top. Cover with tea towel. Let stand in oven with light on and door closed for about 45 minutes until doubled in bulk. Punch dough down. Divide into 4 equal portions. Shape portions into 16 inch (40 cm) long loaves. Make 5 or 6 diagonal shallow scores across top of each loaf. Place on greased baking sheet. Cover with tea towel. Let stand in oven with light on and door closed for 30 minutes. Bake in 400°F (205°C) oven for about 25 minutes until nicely browned. Makes 2 loaves, each cutting into 16 slices.

1 slice: 75 Calories; 1 g Total Fat; 107 mg Sodium; 2 g Protein; 14 g Carbohydrate; 1 g Dietary Fiber

Pictured on page 72.

Suggested fondues: Milky Cheese Fondue, page 76; Tomato Soup Cheese Fondue, page 81.

Mulled Wine

Lightly sweetened red wine with a spicy hint of cloves and cinnamon.
Use whole cinnamon sticks as "spoons" for individual servings.

Dry red (or alcohol-free) wine	3 cups	750 mL
Granulated sugar	1/4 cup	60 mL
Whole cloves	4	4
Cinnamon sticks (about 4 inches, 10 cm, each), broken up	3	3
Thin orange slices	4	4
Thin lemon slices	4	4

Combine all 6 ingredients in medium saucepan. Bring to a simmer. Strain to serve. Discard solids. Makes 3 3/4 cups (925 mL).

1/2 cup (125 mL): 102 Calories; trace Total Fat; 5 mg Sodium; trace Protein; 9 g Carbohydrate; trace Dietary Fiber

Pictured on page 143.

Raspberry Punch

Pretty pink punch that serves a crowd. Garnish individual glasses with quartered orange and lemon slices.

Raspberry ginger ale	8 cups	2 L
Club soda	4 cups	1 L
Fresh (or frozen) raspberries	1 cup	250 mL
Granulated sugar	1/2 cup	125 mL
Thin orange slices	4	4
Thin lemon slices	4	4

Combine all 6 ingredients in large bowl. Stir until sugar is dissolved. Serve immediately. Makes 13 cups (3.25 L).

1 cup (250 mL): 90 Calories; 0.1 g Total Fat; 28 mg Sodium; trace Protein; 23 g Carbohydrate; trace Dietary Fiber

Pictured on front cover.

Measurement Tables

Throughout this book measurements are given in Conventional and Metric measure. To compensate for differences between the two measurements due to rounding, a full metric measure is not always used. The cup used is the standard 8 fluid ounce. Temperature is given in degrees Fahrenheit and Celsius. Baking pan measurements are in inches and centimetres as well as quarts and litres. An exact metric conversion is given below as well as the working equivalent (Metric Standard Measure).

Spoons

Conventional Measure	Metric Exact Conversion Millilitre (mL)	Metric Standard Measure Millilitre (mL)
1/8 teaspoon (tsp.)	0.6 mL	0.5 mL
1/4 teaspoon (tsp.)	1.2 mL	1 mL
1/2 teaspoon (tsp.)	2.4 mL	2 mL
1 teaspoon (tsp.)	4.7 mL	5 mL
2 teaspoons (tsp.)	9.4 mL	10 mL
1 tablespoon (tbsp.)	14.2 mL	15 mL

Cups

Conventional Measure	Metric Exact Conversion Millilitre (mL)	Metric Standard Measure Millilitre (mL)
1/4 cup (4 tbsp.)	56.8 mL	60 mL
1/3 cup (5 1/3 tbsp.)	75.6 mL	75 mL
1/2 cup (8 tbsp.)	113.7 mL	125 mL
2/3 cup (10 2/3 tbsp.)	151.2 mL	150 mL
3/4 cup (12 tbsp.)	170.5 mL	175 mL
1 cup (16 tbsp.)	227.3 mL	250 mL
4 1/2 cups	1022.9 mL	1000 mL (1 L)

Oven Temperatures

Fahrenheit (°F)	Celsius (°C)
175°	80°
200°	95°
225°	110°
250°	120°
275°	140°
300°	150°
325°	160°
350°	175°
375°	190°
400°	205°
425°	220°
450°	230°
475°	240°
500°	260°

Dry Measurements

Conventional Measure Ounces (oz.)	Metric Exact Conversion Grams (g)	Metric Standard Measure Grams (g)
1 oz.	28.3 g	28 g
2 oz.	56.7 g	57 g
3 oz.	85.0 g	85 g
4 oz.	113.4 g	125 g
5 oz.	141.7 g	140 g
6 oz.	170.1 g	170 g
7 oz.	198.4 g	200 g
8 oz.	226.8 g	250 g
16 oz.	453.6 g	500 g
32 oz.	907.2 g	1000 g (1 kg)

Pans

Conventional Inches	Metric Centimetres
8x8 inch	20x20 cm
9x9 inch	22x22 cm
9x13 inch	22x33 cm
10x15 inch	25x38 cm
11x17 inch	28x43 cm
8x2 inch round	20x5 cm
9x2 inch round	22x5 cm
10x4 1/2 inch tube	25x11 cm
8x4x3 inch loaf	20x10x7.5 cm
9x5x3 inch loaf	22x12.5x7.5 cm

Casseroles

CANADA & BRITAIN Standard Size Casserole	Exact Metric Measure	UNITED STATES Standard Size Casserole	Exact Metric Measure
1 qt. (5 cups)	1.13 L	1 qt. (4 cups)	900 mL
1 1/2 qts. (7 1/2 cups)	1.69 L	1 1/2 qts. (6 cups)	1.35 L
2 qts. (10 cups)	2.25 L	2 qts. (8 cups)	1.8 L
2 1/2 qts. (12 1/2 cups)	2.81 L	2 1/2 qts. (10 cups)	2.25 L
3 qts. (15 cups)	3.38 L	3 qts. (12 cups)	2.7 L
4 qts. (20 cups)	4.5 L	4 qts. (16 cups)	3.6 L
5 qts. (25 cups)	5.63 L	5 qts. (20 cups)	4.5 L

Photo Index

A

Aïoli Sauce 54
Apricot Fondue 107

B

Barbecue Sauce 36
Basic Batter 36
Basic Oil Fondue 71
Béarnaise Sauce 71
Beef Dumplings 17
Black Bean Rice Salad 144
Black Currant Fondue 36
Broccoli Cheese Fondue 89

C

Caramel Fondue 108
Cherry Fondue . . . . 125, Back Cover
Chili Bread Fingers 71
Chili Con Queso Fondue . . . . Front Cover
Chocolate Bites 108
Chutney Curry Sauce 18
Crab Dumplings 17
Cracked Pepper Sauce 36
Cranberry Sauce 54
Crêpes Suzette 126
Crispy Rice Dippers . . . . 125, Back Cover

F

Falafels 54
Fresh Herb And Wine Marinade 144
Fried Cheese 18
Fried Rice 143

G

Ginger Marinade 36
Ginger Sauce 35

H

Ham Balls 89
Handy Biscuit Bites 89
Herbed Fondue Bites 89
Herbed Fondue Bread Sticks . . . . Front Cover
Hot Cajun Shrimp 143

L

Ladyfingers 125
Lemon Caper Butter 53

M

Macaroons 107
Marinade For Fish 53

Marinated Tomato And Onion 144
Marmalade Fondue 18
Meatballs 54
Milky Chocolate Fondue . . . 125, Back Cover
Mini-Cakes 108
Mulled Wine 143
Mustard Sauce 54, 71

P

Peanut Butter Cookies . . . . . 125, Back Cover
Pesto Feta Baguette 72
Pineapple Mango Coleslaw 71
Pizza Fondue 90
Plum Sauce 144
Popcorn Clusters 108
Pork Balls 54
Pups In Blankets 36

Q

Quick Batter 53

R

Raisin Honey Sauce 71
Raspberry Punch . . . . Front Cover
Rémoulade Sauce 53
Reuben Gems 18

S

Samosas 54
Seafood Cheese Fondue 72
Sesame Sauce 17
Snappy Black Bean Sauce 17
Spicy Cocktail Sauce 53
Spinach Dumplings 17
Spring Leaf Salad 143
Stone Grill Chicken 144
Strawberry Fondue 107
Sukiyaki Beef 144

T

Tartar Sauce 35
Tempura Fondue 35
Tiny Ginger Cookies . . . . 125, Back Cover
Tiny Puffs 107
Tomato Rarebit Fondue 72

W

Wee Cookies 107
Whole Wheat Focaccia 90

Tip Index

A

Alcohol – to use in flambés 135
Apple – to prevent browning 111
Avoiding spillage – when using a
    fondue pot 27

B

Banana – to prevent browning 111
Batter – to cling better 39
Brandy – to use in flambés 135
Broccoli – cooking in broth or oil fondues . . 21
Broth fondue
    – to cut meat for 33
    – to use as soup base 13
Browning – to prevent in fruit 111

C

Carrots – cooking in broth or oil fondues . . . 21
Cauliflower – cooking in broth or oil
    fondues 21
Ceramic tile – to protect table 27
Cheese fondue – to use leftovers 82
Chicken – to handle safely 123
Contamination – how to avoid 24
Cubed meat – best for oil fondues 33

F

Fish – to avoid contamination 24
    – short marinating time 56
Flambé – how to 135
Flour – to use with batter 39
Fondue burner – to store 117
Fondue fuel – to store 117
Fruit – choosing for fondues 99
    – to prevent browning 111

G

Green onions – cooking in broth or
    oil fondues 21

H

Herbs – to use in preparing meat 23
Hot pad – to protect table 27

L

Leftover cheese fondue – uses for 82
Lemon juice – to use in preventing
    browning 111
Liqueur – to use in flambés 135

M

Marinating – fish and seafood 56
Meat
    – to avoid contamination 24
    – to determine serving size 57
    – to use herbs in preparing 23
    – to use in broth fondues 33
    – to use in oil fondues 33
Mushrooms – cooking in broth or oil
    fondues 21

P

Peppers – cooking in broth or oil fondues . . 21
Potatoes – cooking in broth or oil fondues . . 21
Protecting tabletop 27

R

Rum – to use in flambés 135

S

Seafood – short marinating time 56
Serving size
    – for meat per person 57
    – for vegetables per person 61
Sliced meat – best for broth fondues 33
Soup – to make using leftover cheese
    fondue 82
Soup base – to use broth fondues 13
Spillage – to avoid 27
Sticking – to prevent 29

T

Table surface – to protect 27

V

Vegetables
    – to avoid contamination 24
    – to determine serving size 61
    – which to cook fresh 21
    – which to precook 21

W

Wooden cutting board – to protect table . . . 27

Z

Zucchini – cooking in broth or oil fondues . . 21

Recipe Index

A

A Snap Fondue 24
Aïoli Sauce 56
Appetizer Fondue 95
Apple Kabobs, Pork And 136
Apricot Fondue 104
Asparagus And Crab Soup. . . 128
Avocado Dip, Creamy 58

B

Bacon Blue Cheese Sauce 62
Baguette, Pesto Feta 148
Bangers And Beans Fondue. . . 97
Barbecue Sauce. 52
Basic Batter 38
Basic Beef Fondue 20
Basic Chicken Fondue 20
Basic Fish & Seafood Fondue. . 21
Basic Lamb Fondue 21
Basic Oil Fondue 20
Basic Pork Fondue 21
Basil Garlic Mayo. 64
Batters & Coatings
   Basic Batter. 38
   Crispy Crumb Coating 38
   Crumb Coating. 37
   Fritter Batter 40
   Mustard 22
   Quick Batter 39
   Quick Crumbed Batter 39
   Stuffing Coating 34
   Tempura Batter. 26
Beans
   Bangers And Beans
      Fondue. 97
   Black Bean Rice Salad 145
   Falafels 30
   Snappy Black Bean Sauce . . 60
Béarnaise Sauce. 74
Beef
   Basic Beef Fondue. 20
   Meatballs 23
   Pizza Fondue. 82
   Reuben Gems 22
   Sukiyaki 139
Beef Dumplings. 15
Beef Hot Pot 11
Beer Cheese Fondue 77
Beer Fondue 96
Beer Marinade. 49

Best French Toast 44
Beverages
   Mulled Wine 149
   Raspberry Punch. 149
Biscuit Bites. 88
Biscuit Bites, Handy. 91
Black Bean Rice Salad 145
Black Bean Sauce, Snappy. . . . 60
Black Currant Fondue 112
Blue Cheese Fondue 80
Blue Cheese Sauce, Bacon. . . . 62
Brandied Mocha Fondue. . . . 100
Bread Dippers
   Biscuit Bites. 88
   Chili Bread Fingers 92
   Garlic Dipping Squares 33
   Handy Biscuit Bites 91
   Herbed Fondue Bites. 86
   Herbed Fondue Bread
      Sticks 87
   Savory Puffs 115
   Tiny Puffs 115
   Whole Wheat Focaccia . . . 93
Bread Fingers, Chili 92
Bread Sticks, Herbed Fondue. . 87
Broccoli Cheese Fondue 83
Broth
   Chicken 12
   Easy Chicken. 15
   Rich Chicken. 13
   Spicy. 11
   Vegetable 14
Broth Fondues
   Beef Dumplings 15
   Beef Hot Pot 11
   Crab Dumplings 12
   Ham Balls 19
   Lamb Hot Pot 11
   Pork Balls 16
   Shabu-Shabu For Two. . . . 13
   Spinach Dumplings. 14
Bumbleberry Fondue. 105
Butter, Lemon Caper. 66
Butter Sauce, Madeira 65
Butter Sauce, Orange 133

C

Caesar Seafood Kabobs. 137
Cajun Shrimp, Hot 131
Cakes, Mini- 112
Calamari, Seasoned. 25

Caper Butter, Lemon. 66
Caramel Fondue 110
Caramel Fondue, Chocolate . 102
Chafing Dish
   Asparagus And Crab
      Soup. 128
   Cherries Jubilee. 130
   Coq Au Vin 122
   Hot Chili Cheese Dip 127
   Omelet Supreme 121
   Onion Soup 129
   Orange Butter Sauce. 133
Cheddar Cheese Fondue,
   Sharp 80
Cheese Dip, Hot Chili 127
Cheese Dip, Hot Crab 124
Cheese Fondue Dippers
   Biscuit Bites. 88
   Chili Bread Fingers 92
   Handy Biscuit Bites 91
   Herbed Fondue Bites. 86
   Whole Wheat Focaccia . . . 93
Cheese Fondues
   Beer 77
   Blue 80
   Broccoli. 83
   Chili Con Queso 75
   Emmenthaler 78
   Gruyère. 78
   Herbed 76
   Milky 76
   Neufchâtel 79
   Parmesan 76
   Pizza 82
   Seafood 85
   Sharp Cheddar 80
   Shrimp 87
   Tomato Rarebit 84
   Tomato Soup 81
Cheese, Fried 32
Cheese Sauce, Bacon Blue. . . . 62
Cheese Sauce, Cream 40
Cherries Jubilee 130
Cherry Fondue 106
Cherry Fondue, Mocha 100
Chicken
   Basic Chicken Fondue. . . . 20
   Coq Au Vin 122
   Stone Grill. 140
   Tempura Fondue. 26
Chicken Broth 12

Chicken Broth, Easy 15
Chicken Broth, Rich 13
Chicken Fondue, Basic 20
Chili Bread Fingers 92
Chili Cheese Dip, Hot 127
Chili Con Queso Fondue 75
Chocolate Bites 118
Chocolate Caramel Fondue . . 102
Chocolate Doughnut Holes . . . 43
Chocolate Fondues
    Brandied Mocha 100
    Milky 98
    Mocha Cherry 100
    Peachy White 102
    Peanut Butter 110
    Raspberry 99
    Swiss 103
Chocolate Mint Fondue 101
Chocolate Solo Fondue 101
Chutney Curry Sauce 70
Coatings, see Batters & Coatings
Cocktail Sauce, Spicy 67
Coconut Curry Marinade 50
Coleslaw, Pineapple Mango . 147
Con Queso Fondue, Chili 75
Cookies
    Chocolate Bites 118
    Ladyfingers 116
    Macaroons 113
    Peanut Butter 117
    Tiny Ginger 119
    Tiny Puffs 115
    Wee 114
Coq Au Vin 122
Crab Cheese Dip, Hot 124
Crab Dumplings 12
Crab Soup, Asparagus And . . 128
Cracked Pepper Sauce 51
Cranberry Sauce 68
Cream Cheese Sauce 40
Creamy Avocado Dip 58
Creamy Curry Fondue 96
Creamy Mint Sauce 55
Crêpes 133
Crêpes Suzette 133
Crispy Crumb Coating 38
Crispy Rice Dippers 120
Crumb Coating 37
Crumb Coating, Crispy 38
Crumbed Batter, Quick 39
Cuke Sauce, Yogurt 58
Curry Fondue, Creamy 96
Curry Marinade, Coconut 50
Curry Sauce, Chutney 70

D

Dessert Dippers
    Chocolate Bites 118
    Chocolate Doughnut Holes . 43
    Crispy Rice 120
    Ladyfingers 116
    Macaroons 113
    Maple Bud Pastries 45
    Mini-Cakes 112
    Peanut Butter Cookies 117
    Popcorn Clusters 118
    Quickest Doughnuts 44
    Tiny Ginger Cookies 119
    Tiny Puffs 115
    Wee Cookies 114
Dessert Fondues
    Apricot 104
    Black Currant 112
    Brandied Mocha 100
    Bumbleberry 105
    Caramel 110
    Cherry 106
    Chocolate Caramel 102
    Chocolate Mint 101
    Chocolate Solo 101
    Lemon 109
    Marmalade 111
    Milky Chocolate 98
    Mocha Cherry 100
    Peachy White Chocolate . . 102
    Peanut Butter 110
    Raspberry Chocolate 99
    Strawberry 104
    Swiss Chocolate 103
Dilly-Of-A-Dipping Sauce 67
Dippers, see Bread Dippers or
    Dessert Dippers
Dipping Sauces, Savory
    Aïoli 56
    Bacon Blue Cheese 62
    Barbecue 52
    Basil Garlic Mayo 64
    Béarnaise 74
    Chutney Curry 70
    Cracked Pepper 51
    Creamy Avocado 58
    Creamy Mint 55
    Dilly-Of-A- 67
    Ginger 69
    Italian 62
    Kickin' Hot 57
    Lemon Caper Butter 66
    Madeira Butter 65
    Mustard 64
    Niçoise 63

Rémoulade 59
Sesame 69
Snappy Black Bean 60
Spicy Cocktail 67
Tartar 66
Teriyaki 61
Yogurt Cuke 58
Dipping Sauces, Sweet
    Black Currant Fondue 112
    Cranberry 68
    Cream Cheese 40
    Marmalade Fondue 111
    Orange 60
    Plum 68
    Raisin Honey 73
Dips
    Creamy Avocado 58
    Hot Chili Cheese 127
    Hot Crab Cheese 124
Doughnut Holes, Chocolate . . 43
Doughnuts, Quickest 44
Dressing, Oil And Vinegar . . . 142
Dressing, Pineapple 147
Dressing, Walnut 146
Dumplings
    Beef 15
    Crab 12
    Spinach 14

E

Easy Chicken Broth 15
Emmenthaler Fondue 78

F

Falafels 30
Feta Baguette, Pesto 148
Fish & Seafood
    A Snap Fondue 24
    Asparagus And Crab Soup 128
    Basic Fish & Seafood
        Fondue 21
    Caesar Seafood Kabobs . . . 137
    Crab Dumplings 12
    Hot Cajun Shrimp 131
    Hot Crab Cheese Dip 124
    Marinade For 46
    Seafood Cheese Fondue . . . 85
    Seasoned Calamari 25
    Shrimp And Scallop
        Newburg 134
    Shrimp Cheese Fondue 87
    Tempura Fondue 26
Flambé Pan
    Crêpes Suzette 133
    Ham And Mushroom
        Mounds 132

154

Hot Cajun Shrimp 131
Hot Crab Cheese Dip 124
Shrimp And Scallop
    Newburg 134
Focaccia, Whole Wheat 93
French Toast, Best 44
Fresh Herb And Wine
    Marinade 50
Fried Cheese 32
Fried Rice 141
Fritter Batter 40
Fruit Filling 42
Fruit Fondues
    Apricot 104
    Black Currant 112
    Bumbleberry 105
    Cherry 106
    Lemon 109
    Marmalade 111
    Strawberry 104
    Tropical 40
Fruit Packets 41
Fruit Pies, Perogy 42

G

Garlic Dipping Squares 33
Garlic Mayo, Basil 64
Ginger Cookies, Tiny 119
Ginger Marinade 49
Ginger Sauce 69
Go-Withs
    Black Bean Rice Salad 145
    Fried Rice 141
    Marinated Tomato And
        Onion 142
    Mulled Wine 149
    Pesto Feta Baguette 148
    Pineapple Dressing 147
    Pineapple Mango
        Coleslaw 147
    Raspberry Punch 149
    Spring Leaf Salad 146
    Walnut Dressing 146
Gruyère Fondue 78

H

Ham And Mushroom
    Mounds 132
Ham Balls 19
Handy Biscuit Bites 91
Herb And Wine Marinade,
    Fresh 50
Herbed Cheese Fondue 76
Herbed Fondue Bites 86
Herbed Fondue Bread Sticks . . 87
Honey Sauce, Raisin 73

Hot Cajun Shrimp 131
Hot Chili Cheese Dip 127
Hot Crab Cheese Dip 124
Hot Pots
    Beef 11
    Lamb 11
Hot Sauce, Kickin' 57

I

Italian Sauce 62

K

Kabobs
    Caesar Seafood 137
    Lamb-On-A-Stick 138
    Pork And Apple 136
    Sukiyaki Beef 139
Kickin' Hot Sauce 57

L

Ladyfingers 116
Lamb Fondue, Basic 21
Lamb Hot Pot 11
Lamb-On-A-Stick 138
Lemon Caper Butter 66
Lemon Fondue 109

M

Macaroons 113
Madeira Butter Sauce 65
Mango Coleslaw, Pineapple . 147
Maple Bud Pastries 45
Marinade For Fish 46
Marinades
    Beer 49
    Coconut Curry 50
    Fresh Herb And Wine 50
    Ginger 49
    Pepper 48
    Robust Red Wine 47
    Teriyaki 48
    White Wine 47
Marinated Tomato And
    Onion 142
Marmalade Fondue 111
Meatballs 23
Milky Cheese Fondue 76
Milky Chocolate Fondue 98
Mini-Cakes 112
Mint Fondue, Chocolate 101
Mint Sauce, Creamy 55
Mixed Veggies 31
Mocha Cherry Fondue 100
Mocha Fondue, Brandied . . . 100
Mulled Wine 149

Mushroom Mounds, Ham
    And 132
Mustard Coating 22
Mustard Sauce 64

N

Neufchâtel Cheese Fondue . . . 79
Newburg, Shrimp And
    Scallop 134
Niçoise Sauce 63

O

Oil And Vinegar Dressing . . . 142
Oil Fondues
    A Snap 24
    Basic 20
    Basic Beef 20
    Basic Chicken 20
    Basic Fish And Seafood 21
    Basic Lamb 21
    Basic Pork 21
    Best French Toast 44
    Chocolate Doughnut Holes . 43
    Falafels 30
    Fried Cheese 32
    Fruit Packets 41
    Garlic Dipping Squares 33
    Maple Bud Pastries 45
    Meatballs 23
    Mixed Veggies 31
    Perogy Fruit Pies 42
    Potato Skins 27
    Pups In Blankets 29
    Quickest Doughnuts 44
    Reuben Gems 22
    Samosas 28
    Seasoned Calamari 25
    Tempura 26
    Tropical 40
Omelet Supreme 121
Onion, Marinated Tomato
    And 142
Onion Soup 129
Orange Butter Sauce 133
Orange Sauce 60

P

Parmesan Fondue 76
Peachy White Chocolate
    Fondue 102
Peanut Butter Cookies 117
Peanut Butter Fondue 110
Pepper Marinade 48
Pepper Sauce, Cracked 51
Perogy Fruit Pies 42
Pesto Feta Baguette 148

155

Pies, Perogy Fruit. 42
Pineapple Dressing 147
Pineapple Mango Coleslaw. . 147
Pizza Fondue. 82
Plum Sauce. 68
Popcorn Clusters. 118
Pork
    Basic Pork Fondue. 21
    Ham And Mushroom
        Mounds 132
    Ham Balls 19
    Omelet Supreme 121
    Pups In Blankets 29
Pork And Apple Kabobs. 136
Pork Balls. 16
Potato Skins 27
Punch, Raspberry 149
Pups In Blankets 29

Q

Quick Batter 39
Quick Crumbed Batter 39
Quickest Doughnuts 44

R

Raisin Honey Sauce. 73
Rarebit Fondue, Tomato 84
Raspberry Chocolate Fondue. . 99
Raspberry Punch. 149
Red Wine Marinade, Robust . . 47
Rémoulade Sauce 59
Reuben Gems 22
Rice Dippers, Crispy 120
Rice, Fried. 141
Rice Salad, Black Bean. 145
Rich Chicken Broth 13
Robust Red Wine Marinade. . . 47

S

Salads
    Black Bean Rice. 145
    Marinated Tomato And
        Onion. 142
    Pineapple Mango
        Coleslaw. 147
    Spring Leaf 146
Samosas 28
Sauce Fondues, Savory
    Appetizer 95
    Bangers And Beans. 97
    Beer 96
    Creamy Curry. 96
    Sweet And Sour 94
Sauce Fondues, Sweet, see
    Dessert Fondues

Sauce, Orange Butter 133
Sauces, see Dipping Sauces
Savory Puffs 115
Scallops
    Caesar Seafood Kabobs. . . 137
    Shrimp And Scallop
        Newburg 134
Seafood Cheese Fondue 85
Seafood Fondue, Basic Fish &. . 21
Seafood Kabobs, Caesar 137
Seafood, see Fish & Seafood
Seasoned Calamari 25
Sesame Sauce 69
Shabu-Shabu For Two. 13
Sharp Cheddar Cheese
    Fondue. 80
Shrimp
    Caesar Seafood Kabobs. . . 137
    Hot Cajun 131
Shrimp And Scallop
    Newburg 134
Shrimp Cheese Fondue. 87
Snap Fondue, A. 24
Snappy Black Bean Sauce 60
Soup, Asparagus And Crab . . 128
Soup Cheese Fondue,
    Tomato. 81
Soup, Onion 129
Spicy Broth 11
Spicy Cocktail Sauce 67
Spinach Dumplings. 14
Spring Leaf Salad 146
Stone Grill
    Caesar Seafood Kabobs. . . 137
    Lamb-On-A Stick. 138
    Pork And Apple Kabobs . . 136
    Sukiyaki Beef. 139
Stone Grill Chicken 140
Strawberry Fondue 104
Stuffing Coating 34
Sukiyaki Beef. 139
Sweet And Sour Fondue 94
Swiss Chocolate Fondue 103

T

Tabletop Cooking
    Asparagus And Crab Soup 128
    Caesar Seafood Kabobs. . . 137
    Cherries Jubilee. 130
    Coq Au Vin 122
    Crêpes Suzette 133
    Ham And Mushroom
        Mounds 132
    Hot Cajun Shrimp. 131
    Hot Chili Cheese Dip 127

Hot Crab Cheese Dip 124
Lamb-On-A-Stick. 138
Omelet Supreme 121
Onion Soup 129
Pork And Apple Kabobs . . 136
Shrimp And Scallop
    Newburg 134
Stone Grill Chicken 140
Sukiyaki Beef. 139
Tartar Sauce 66
Tempura Batter. 26
Tempura Fondue. 26
Teriyaki Marinade 48
Teriyaki Sauce 61
Tiny Ginger Cookies 119
Tiny Puffs 115
Toast, Best French 44
Tomato And Onion,
    Marinated. 142
Tomato Rarebit Fondue. 84
Tomato Soup Cheese Fondue . 81
Tropical Fondue 40

V

Vegetable Broth 14
Vegetables
    Falafels 30
    Marinated Tomato And
        Onion. 142
    Mixed Veggies 31
    Potato Skins 27
    Samosas 28
    Tempura Fondue. 26
Vinegar Dressing, Oil And . . . 142

W

Walnut Dressing 146
Wee Cookies. 114
White Chocolate Fondue,
    Peachy 102
White Wine Marinade 47
Whole Wheat Focaccia 93
Wieners
    Pups In Blankets 29
Wine Marinades
    Fresh Herb And. 50
    Robust Red 47
    White 47
Wine, Mulled. 149

Y

Yogurt Cuke Sauce 58

Company's Coming cookbooks are available at retail locations throughout Canada!

EXCLUSIVE mail order offer on next page
Buy any 2 cookbooks—choose a 3rd FREE of equal or lesser value than the lowest price paid.

Original Series — CA$15.99 Canada — US$12.99 USA & International

CODE		CODE		CODE	
SQ	150 Delicious Squares	CFK	Cook For Kids	WM	30-Minute Weekday Meals
CA	Casseroles	SCH	Stews, Chilies & Chowders	SDL	School Days Lunches
MU	Muffins & More	FD	Fondues	PD	Potluck Dishes
SA	Salads	CCBE	The Beef Book	GBR	Ground Beef Recipes
AP	Appetizers	RC	The Rookie Cook	FRIR	4-Ingredient Recipes
SS	Soups & Sandwiches	RHR	Rush-Hour Recipes	KHC	Kids' Healthy Cooking
CO	Cookies	SW	Sweet Cravings	MM	Mostly Muffins
PA	Pasta	YRG	Year-Round Grilling	SP	Soups
BA	Barbecues	GG	Garden Greens	SU	Simple Suppers
PR	Preserves	CHC	Chinese Cooking	CCDC	Diabetic Cooking
CH	Chicken, Etc.	PK	The Pork Book	CHN	Chicken Now
CT	Cooking For Two	RL	Recipes For Leftovers	KDS	Kids Do Snacks
SC	Slow Cooker Recipes	EB	The Egg Book		**NEW** July 1/07
SF	Stir-Fry	SDPP	School Days Party Pack		
MAM	Make-Ahead Meals	HS	Herbs & Spices		
PB	The Potato Book	BEV	The Beverage Book		
CLFC	Low-Fat Cooking	SCD	Slow Cooker Dinners		

Cookbook Author Biography

CODE	CA$15.99 Canada US$12.99 USA & International
JP	Jean Paré: An Appetite for Life

Most Loved Recipe Collection

CODE	CA$23.99 Canada US$19.99 USA & International
MLA	Most Loved Appetizers
LMC	Most Loved Main Courses
MLT	Most Loved Treats
LBQ	Most Loved Barbecuing
LCO	Most Loved Cookies

CODE	CA$24.99 Canada US$19.99 USA & International
LSD	Most Loved Salads & Dressings
LCA	Most Loved Casseroles
LSF	Most Loved Stir-Fries

3-in-1 Cookbook Collection

CODE	CA$29.99 Canada US$24.99 USA & International
EE	Quick & Easy Entertaining
NT	Meals in No Time

Lifestyle Series

CODE	CA$17.99 Canada US$15.99 USA & International
DC	Diabetic Cooking

CODE	CA$19.99 Canada US$15.99 USA & International
DDI	Diabetic Dinners
LCR	Low-Carb Recipes
HR	Easy Healthy Recipes
HH	Healthy in a Hurry
WGR	Whole Grain Recipes
	NEW August 1/07

Special Occasion Series

CODE	CA$20.99 Canada US$19.99 USA & International
GFK	Gifts from the Kitchen

CODE	CA$24.99 Canada US$19.99 USA & International
BSS	Baking—Simple to Sensational
CGFK	Christmas Gifts from the Kitchen
TR	Timeless Recipes for All Occasions

CODE	CA$27.99 Canada US$22.99 USA & International
CCEL	Christmas Celebrations

Order **ONLINE** for fast delivery!

Log onto **www.companyscoming.com**, browse through our library of cookbooks, gift sets and newest releases and place your order using our fast and secure online order form.

Buy 2, Get 1 FREE!

Buy any 2 cookbooks—choose a **3rd FREE** of equal or lesser value than the lowest price paid.

Title	Code	Quantity	Price	Total
			$	$
DON'T FORGET				
to indicate your FREE BOOK(S).				
(see exclusive mail order offer above)				
please print				

TOTAL BOOKS (including FREE)

TOTAL BOOKS PURCHASED: $

	International	USA	Canada
Shipping & Handling First Book (per destination)	$ 11.98 (one book)	$ 6.98 (one book)	$ 5.98 (one book)
Additional Books (include FREE books)	$ ($4.99 each)	$ ($1.99 each)	$ ($1.99 each)
Sub-Total	$	$	$
Canadian residents add GST/HST			$
TOTAL AMOUNT ENCLOSED	$	$	$

Terms

- All orders must be prepaid. Sorry, no CODs.
- Prices are listed in Canadian Funds for Canadian orders, or US funds for US & International orders.
- Prices are subject to change without prior notice.
- Canadian residents must pay GST/HST (no provincial tax required).
- No tax is required for orders outside Canada.
- Satisfaction is guaranteed or return within 30 days for a full refund.
- Make cheque or money order payable to: **Company's Coming Publishing Limited** 2311-96 Street, Edmonton, Alberta Canada T6N 1G3.
- Orders are shipped surface mail. For courier rates, visit our website: **www.companyscoming.com** or contact us: **Tel: 780-450-6223 Fax: 780-450-1857.**

Gift Giving

- Let us help you with your gift giving!
- We will send cookbooks directly to the recipients of your choice if you give us their names and addresses.
- Please specify the titles you wish to send to each person.
- If you would like to include a personal note or card, we will be pleased to enclose it with your gift order.
- Company's Coming Cookbooks make excellent gifts: birthdays, bridal showers, Mother's Day, Father's Day, graduation or any occasion ...collect them all!

☐ MasterCard ☐ VISA Expiry ____ / ____ MO/YR

Credit Card # _____

Name of cardholder _____

Cardholder signature _____

Shipping Address Send the cookbooks listed above to:

☐ **Please check if this is a Gift Order**

Name: _____

Street: _____

City: _____ Prov./State: _____

Postal Code/Zip: _____ Country: _____

Tel: (___) _____

E-mail address: _____

Your privacy is important to us. We will not share your e-mail address or personal information with any outside par

☐ **YES! Please add me to your News Bite e-mail newsletter**

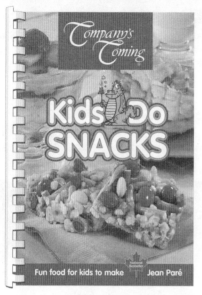

Know a budding chef who's eager to cook? Company's Coming presents *Kids Do Snacks*—a fun cookbook that lets kids become the masters of the kitchen. From *Blend It!* to *Bake It!*, the chapters are arranged so young cooks-in-training can learn more and more tricks and techniques as they go along—making it suitable for kids of all skill levels.

COOKBOOKS

Quick & Easy Recipes

Everyday Ingredients

Canada's **most popular cookbooks!**